# AN INTRODUCTION
# TO MENTAL PHILOSOPHY.

# AN INTRODUCTION TO MENTAL PHILOSOPHY.

## IN TWO PARTS.

INTENDED ESPECIALLY FOR THE USE OF STUDENTS IN UNIVERSITIES.

IN PART SECOND IS CONTAINED

A PARTICULAR INQUIRY INTO THE NATURE AND VALUE OF THE SYLLOGISM.

### BY GEORGE RAMSAY, B. M.

AUTHOR OF "AN ESSAY ON THE DISTRIBUTION OF WEALTH,"
"ANALYSIS AND THEORY OF THE EMOTIONS,"
"A CLASSIFICATION OF THE SCIENCES,"
ETC. ETC.

EDINBURGH: ADAM AND CHARLES BLACK.
LONDON: LONGMAN, BROWN, GREEN, AND LONGMANS.
RUGBY: CROSSLEY AND BILLINGTON.

M.D.CCC.LIII.

L'homme n'est qu'un roseau le plus faible de la nature, mais c'est un roseau pensant.

Toute la dignité de l'homme est en la pensée.—Pascal.

# PREFACE.

THE attempt made in the following pages to determine the meaning of some of the principal terms employed in Philosophy, may, to some, appear an ambitious undertaking; while, to others, it may seem merely a verbal affair. If to emulate the " Great of old" be ambition, to that the author must plead guilty; for Aristotle himself composed a Philosophical Vocabulary; and, on the other hand, that the object of such a work is useful and dignified, will be allowed by those who are best acquainted with the difficulties of Philosophy. I may mention in particular two distinguished philosophers of the present day, who have thus expressed themselves on this subject.

Dr. Whewell observes, that "Discussions and speculations concerning the import of very abstract and general terms and notions, may be, and in reality have been, far from useless and barren. Such discussions arose from the desire of men to impress their opinions on others, but they had the effect of making the opinions much more clear and distinct. In trying to make others understand them they learnt to understand themselves. Their speculations were begun in twilight, and ended in the full brilliancy of day."*

Again, Mr. Mill remarks, that "Although according to the views here presented, Definitions are of Names only, and not of Things, it does not follow that definition is an easy matter. How to define a Name, may not only be an inquiry of considerable difficulty and intricacy, but may turn upon considerations going deep into the nature of the things which are denoted by the Name. Such, for instance, are the inquiries

* "Philosophy of the Inductive Sciences," Part II. Book xi. Chap. 2.

which form the subject of the most important of Plato's dialogues. * * * * * *
It would be a mistake to represent these difficult and noble inquiries as having nothing in view beyond ascertaining the conventional meaning of a Name. They are inquiries not so much to determine what is, as what should be, the meaning of a Name; which, like other practical questions of terminology, requires for its solution, that we should enter, and sometimes very deeply, into the properties, not merely of names, but of the things named."*

The part of the work likely to meet with the most opposition is that wherein are discussed the *nature* and *value* of the SYLLOGISM. The importance of correct opinions on this subject; the long, and still fondly cherished errors, as I conceive, concerning it; the great names, from Aristotle down even to the present day, arrayed against me; the authority and teaching of one venerable University; all induced me to devote patient and oft repeated thought to this question.

* System of Logic, Book I. Chap. viii. Sec. 8.

Well pleased, indeed, should I be, could I have arrived at a conclusion supported by some of the first men of our times; and sorry above all am I to oppose the deep convictions of ONE EMINENT MAN, whom I rejoice to call a friend: but, my apology shall be given in the words of his favourite author, Aristotle; words adopted as his own; namely, "That a philosopher, *a lover of wisdom,* is bound in the cause of Truth, to refute all error, be it the error of himself or of his friends; for though friends be dear, it is still his hallowed duty to give the higher reverence to Truth." To that sentiment I fully subscribe; and I feel confident that nothing here said will interrupt for one moment that friendly intercourse which has so long subsisted between us, and which, by me, has ever been considered as a pleasure, a profit, and a privilege.

RUGBY, NOVEMBER, 1852.

# CONTENTS.

## PART FIRST.

### PHILOSOPHICAL VOCABULARY.

| | | |
|---|---|---|
| I. | SUBSTANCE: | |
| | MIND OR SPIRIT, BODY OR MATTER | 1 |
| II. | QUALITY | 6 |
| III. | QUANTITY | 14 |
| IV. | RELATION | 27 |
| V. | POWER, CAUSE AND EFFECT | 40 |
| VI. | LAW | 55 |
| VII. | LAW OF NATURE: | |
| | EXPLANATION OF PHENOMENA | 58 |
| VIII. | PRINCIPLE | 65 |
| IX. | A REASON | 73 |
| X. | SCIENCE AND PHILOSOPHY | 76 |
| XI. | HYPOTHESIS AND THEORY | 95 |
| XII. | METAPHYSICS, LOGIC, GRAMMAR: | |
| | THEIR RESPECTIVE PROVINCES | 104 |

## Part Second.

| | | |
|---|---|---|
| I. | The Categories | 131 |
| II. | Proposition,—The Predicables | 145 |
| | 1. Definition of a Proposition | 145 |
| | 2. What things are signified by the terms of a Proposition | 151 |
| | 3. What we affirm or deny concerning these things | 161 |
| III. | Reasoning | 176 |
| | 1. Reasoning in general | 177 |
| | 2. Demonstrative Reasoning | 179 |
| | 3. Probable Reasoning | 184 |
| |     Inductive and Deductive Reasoning | 184 |
| |     Plain Reasoning | 219 |
| | 4. The Syllogism | 220 |
| | 5. Different Relations traced by different sorts of Reasoning | 254 |
| | 6. General Principles of Reasoning | 257 |

# AN INTRODUCTION

# TO MENTAL PHILOSOPHY.

# PHILOSOPHICAL VOCABULARY.

## SUBSTANCE.

SUBSTANCE is a word applied to two things, apparently as different as any can be, namely, Matter and Mind, or Body and Spirit. But in spite of this great difference, there must be some resemblance, however faint; otherwise a common name would hardly have been given to them. What, then, is this circumstance belonging to both, on account of which each is called a Substance? This, it would appear, is nothing but *Permanence*—permanence amid innumerable changes or modifications. Matter may undergo very great changes; from a solid it may become a liquid; from a liquid, an air or gas; or two gases may unite, and in so doing may lose their own properties; or acids, with alkalis, may form neutral salts; but something still remains constant. So the Mind may pass through an innumerable variety of conditions—far more than we can express in words; such as Sensations, Thoughts, Emotions, which comprise vast classes of phenomena; but, through all this variety, there is something fixed or permanent. It is on this account we conceive that the term SUBSTANCE has been applied to both Mind and Body. A Substance, then, may be defined as *something permanent or constant amid innumerable modifications.*

From the above it appears that, widely different as the Substances, Matter and Mind, undoubtedly are, there are still things more different. Such are Mind, and the modifications of Matter or its qualities; Matter, and the modifications or qualities, and the phenomena of Mind, for these have not even the common property of permanence or constancy; and consequently they have no common name.

Substance is a *genus* comprehending two *species*, MIND or SPIRIT, and BODY or MATTER. So far as each is a Substance they have something in common; but by what differences are they separated?

Matter has sometimes been defined as the outward and unknown cause of our Sensations; but when we come to enquire what is a Sensation, we say that it is a Mental phenomenon, of which the cause, or at least the invariable antecedent, is some change in the state of our body. Hence Matter, or Body, is defined as the cause of Sensation, and Sensation as the Effect of Body, or we define in a circle. Let us then see whether we have not some less vague notion of Matter.

Matter certainly gives occasion in us to innumerable sensations, and notions consequent thereon; and there are a few of these sensations and notions which we never fail to experience whenever Matter is present, and on which, therefore, we have fixed as serving to distinguish it from other things. But in this case it is not on the sensations that we fix, but on the notions thence derived; the former being quite overlooked.

Thus, *first*, all Matter gives us the notion of *Extension*, and therefore we say that all Matter is extended, and thus we distinguish it from Spirit. *Secondly*, all Matter gives us the notion of *Solidity* or *Impenetrability*; which means that it fills space, or that two bodies cannot occupy the same space at the same time. Thus is Matter distinguished from simple Extension.

Now, our notion of Matter always comprehends these two notions, together with the notion of Substance before stated; and from these we cannot doubt that it originated; and we think from these alone, and not from colour, sound, or taste. As for the two latter, we can conceive Matter without them at all; and, indeed, there are not a few born deaf who yet know Matter; and we cannot suppose that a mere want of taste would be attended by a total ignorance of the world without. Nay, there have been children born deaf, dumb, and blind, who yet were acquainted with Matter. If this be so, the notion of Matter does not necessarily embrace colour, and was certainly not derived from it, though those who enjoy sight may not, from constant association, easily abstract colour from Matter. The power of conceiving a thing without another thing is a proof that the conception of the former is independent of the conception of the latter; but our inability to conceive the one without the other is no proof that the two conceptions are necessarily inseparable; for the inability may be owing to long continued association.

From the above it follows that Matter may be defined to be *an Extended Solid Substance*. Spirit, on the other hand, is supposed neither to be extended nor solid, but its existence is known to us from the various mental phenomena of which we are conscious,—Sensations, Thoughts, Emotions. Amid the constant and rapid succession of these phenomena, we cannot help believing that there is something permanent, which is therefore a Substance, and which I call Self. The existence of this substance is more intimately known, is brought more home to us; in other words, is known more immediately than that of Matter, for the former is known by phenomena which are states of its own being; the latter through the medium of those mental states, called sensations, which are totally distinct from matter itself.

From all this it appears that spirit may be defined to be *a Substance, neither extended nor solid, but susceptible of Sensations, Thoughts, and Emotions.*

Here it is not said that the word Spirit, or Mind, implies a Substance which at all times thinks or feels, for it is a disputed point whether or not there be always some consciousness, as in deep sleep, or in a swoon; but we should never give the name of Mind to that which either had never been conscious, or which had ceased to be capable of consciousness. It is then the capability which the term implies, and not the constant exercise of that capability.

## QUALITY.

The word Substance, simply signifying permanent existence, seems to be one out of a very small number of terms which are strictly non-relative. Not so QUALITY, which is synonymous with POWER, and implies the relation of cause and effect. All our knowledge of Matter is derived from its effects upon us; that is, from our sensations; and all our knowledge of Spirit is obtained from its own sensations, thoughts, and emotions; and though these sensations, thoughts, and emotions, be ever changing, yet we believe not only that there is something permanent which gives rise to them all, and which in the one case we call Matter, in the other Mind, but also that each sensation, thought, and emotion, has a peculiar permanent cause, either external or internal, material or mental; and this we call a Quality. But as our experience tells us that outward objects, as well as our own minds, undergo, in the course of time, considerable changes: we do not attach the same degree of permanence to a Quality as to Matter or Mind itself. The Quality, however, is nothing distinct from Matter or Mind: it is one or the other in a certain state;—in other words, it is a modification of either, less constant than Substance—more so than a mere phenomenon. When I experience a sensation of redness, I say that the object before me is red, or has the quality of redness; meaning that I believe that the cause of the sensation is an outward object, and that the object which now affects me thus will always affect me in like manner (my eyesight and my distance from the object remaining the same); and not me only, but all persons similarly situated. I can clearly distinguish between the passing sensation of redness and the cause, which I believe to be permanent, and which for a thousand years may arouse similar sensations in successive generations of men. But wind, rain, or other casualties, may in time change the colour from red to black, or entirely alter the figure, or even the intimate nature of the object; and it is conceivable that our sensations from the same object may vary; and consequently a Quality has not necessarily the permanence of simple substance. Substance has been defined to be something permanent among innumerable modifications. Now these modifications are either qualities or phenomena, and the former are permanent as compared with the latter. But were all animated nature at once destroyed, there would be an end to the qualities of matter, *as we comprehend them;* because Quality supposes two things—an outward object and a percipient mind; though there might still be Substance.

This account of Quality agrees perfectly with the doctrine of Locke, contained in the following passage. And I am the more desirous of quoting that passage, because the opinions of Locke have been so much misrepresented, and this subject in particular has been so much mystified by succeeding writers:—" Whatever the mind perceives in itself, or is the immediate object of perception, thought, or understanding, that I call *Idea;* and the power to produce any idea in our mind I call *Quality* of the subject wherein that power is. Thus a snowball, having the power to produce in us the idea of white, cold, and round, the power to produce those ideas in us as they are in the snowball I call *Qualities;* and as they are sensations or perceptions in our understandings, I call them *ideas;* which ideas, if I speak of them sometimes as in the things themselves, I would be understood to mean those qualities in the objects which produce them in us."—*Essay concerning Human Understanding,* Book ii. chap. viii. sec. 8. See also sec. 2.

Had Locke written nothing more on the subject of Quality than this section, it seems impossible that his opinions could have been misunderstood; and we can attribute the disputes which have arisen with respect to him, only to some unguarded expressions in the remainder of the chapter, and in particular to his observations on primary and secondary Qualities. "From whence I think it is easy to draw this observation, that the ideas of primary qualities of bodies, are resemblances of them, and their patterns do really exist in the bodies themselves, but the ideas produced in us by these secondary qualities have no resemblance to them at all. There is nothing like our ideas existing in the bodies themselves. They are, in the bodies we denominate from them, only a power to produce those sensations in us; and what is sweet, blue, or warm in idea, is but the certain bulk, figure, and motion, of the insensible parts in the bodies themselves, which we call so." Sec. 15.

This distinction does not seem well founded. The ideas of primary qualities no more resemble the qualities themselves, than the ideas of secondary qualities resemble these. The quality, the cause, is always external; the idea, the effect resulting from it, always internal, and the one can bear no resemblance to the other; the former appertaining to Matter, the latter to Mind. The secondary quality is quite as real as the primary, and we have quite as much reason to believe the one as the other. Either both exist outwardly, or neither. We are as firmly convinced that there exists something without, the cause of the sensation of blueness, as we are that there is an outward cause of the sensation of resistance.

Nevertheless, there is a good distinction between the primary and secondary qualities of Matter, and it consists in this, that the former alone are sufficient to constitute what Locke calls the *Nominal Essence;* in other words, sufficient to our notion of matter; so that wherever these qualities exist, there we say is Matter, and wherever these qualities exist not, there we say is none. The primary qualities, then, are those to the union of which we have given the name *Matter*, and the statement of them is the definition of this term. Of course then they must be inseparable from matter, under all its modifications, for were they not present, we should not apply the name. When we say that they constitute our notion of Matter, we imply that they are inseparable from it; and afterwards to state that they are so, is a truism, and nothing more.

What those qualities are which are sufficient to induce us to give the name of Matter, we have already seen. They are Extension and Solidity, or Impenetrability. All other qualities are secondary, for they do not of necessity enter into our notions of a material substance. Bodies may be without colour, as in the dark; without sound, as in a vacuum; without smell, without taste, but still they are Matter.

It is, no doubt, very difficult, for us who see, to conceive Matter without colour, but this is only the result of constant association, for we know that those born blind are acquainted with colourless Matter. A druggist or apothecary cannot easily conceive senna apart from its purgative effect; but a botanist is wholly taken up with the marks which determine its class, order, genus, and species, and thinks not at all of its medicinal virtues. Facility or difficulty of conception, then, proves only frequency or infrequency of association, and is no test of what is required and alone required: in other words, of what is sufficient or essential to our notion of that thing to which we give a name, whether it be Matter or any other.

There is another division of Qualities which deserves to be attended to, viz., that into Simple and Relative. The Simple Qualities of bodies are those which affect our senses, without changing other bodies, as redness, blueness, hardness, softness, roughness, smoothness, &c., smells and tastes, &c.

The Relative Qualities are such as first change other bodies, and then operate anew upon our senses, as an acid, which changes a vegetable blue to red, or by mixing with an alkali, produces a new substance, a salt; or as fire, which melts lead, or causes the explosion of gunpowder. Though this distinction be well founded, yet we must not suppose that Simple Qualities involve no relation. They certainly imply a relation between the outward object and the percipient mind, for when we say that blood is red, or has the quality of redness, we mean that it is a substance which rouses in us a sensation of redness. But Relative Qualities imply no less than four relations. To take the case of an acid uniting with an alkali to form a salt: there is first the simple relation between the acid and our percipient mind; secondly, the relation between the alkali and our mind; thirdly, the relation between the acid and the alkali, resulting in a mutual transformation; which third relation is known to us by a fourth, that between the new product, a salt, and our mind which perceives it. Therefore, there is a well-marked distinction between Simple and Relative Qualities, and the names seem sufficiently well chosen for the purpose; the one set of Qualities being so much more simple than the other.

The word ATTRIBUTE seems to be nearly, if not quite, synonymous with QUALITY, only it is not so often used in reference to Body, being mostly confined to Spirit, and often applied in particular to that Great Spirit which created and governs the universe.

Attribute of mind, like Quality of body, means something less constant than Simple Substance, more so than a mere phenomenon, and yet not distinct from substance any more than phenomenon is; but only that substance existing, not in any state whatever, for then it would be simply substance; nor yet in a fleeting state, for then it would be merely phenomenon; but in a state which may be called habitual, being apt to recur, and to continue for some time. An Attribute may, therefore, be defined as *an habitual state of mind.* The assemblage of the *moral* Attributes is called the *disposition*.

* For other meanings of the word *Attribute*, and in particular the distinction between the logical and the metaphysical sense, see the article on the Categories. Part ii. Art. 1.

## QUANTITY.

The word QUALITY necessarily implies Substance, mental or bodily; for a quality is nothing but a substance, existing in such a state as to render us conscious of its existence, whether by means of sensation, as in the case of body, or of any mental phenomenon whatsoever, as in the case of Mind. Quality, then, is inseparable from Substance; but not so QUANTITY: for time and space have Quantity, since we understand what we say when we talk of the length of a mile or of a day, and neither time nor space necessarily imply Substance. And though Quantity belongs to all Bodies, yet is it not peculiar to *Body*; for neither time nor space is material. To know, then, what is meant by Quantity, we must consider it where it exists with the least possible complication with other things.

Since Quantity belongs to both space and time, these have something in common. But what is that something? Time and space agree in this, and in this only, that they have parts, and are capable of increase or diminution, by the addition or the subtraction of the parts; and this addition or subtraction may go on to infinity, in other words, without any limit which we can assign. Who can set bounds to the multiplication or division of miles or of years? Quantity, then, being that which is common to space and time, means this capability? When a thing can be increased or diminished *ad infinitum*, by adding or subtracting similar parts, there is Quantity; but where it cannot be so increased or diminished, there we have Quality, which admits of *Shades*, or degrees, not accurately fixed, and that soon find a limit. Thus we talk of degrees of excellence in tastes, degrees of hardness and softness, the shades of colour, or of good and evil, &c. &c.

In all these we soon reach a limit, beyond which if we attempt to go, we change the Quality into something else. What is whiter than snow? Do we attempt to produce greater whiteness, we change it altogether.

Quantity, on the contrary, has no *Shades*, because one Quantity is perfectly distinct from every other, and no limit. Shades suppose gradual and insensible approximation, and hence indistinctness; but *one* is as distinct from *two* as *from two thousand*.

This is the reason why the relations of Quantity alone admit of demonstration. Here every difference is distinct; whereas, in other things, each difference is not distinct. Therefore Morality does not admit of demonstration, as Locke supposes. The shades of action are innumerable, and indistinctly marked. In questions respecting Quantity there is but one alternative,—either a thing is, or it is not; but in all other subjects there may be a middle term, or many middle terms, partaking of the character of the two opposites. Either the two angles of a triangle are equal to two right angles, or they are not: but who shall say that one form of government is always good, another always bad; that one line of policy, or one mode of action, is invariably the best, another always the worst? These very words, *best* and *worst*, suppose many intervening degrees of goodness. Quantity, then, is the subject of demonstrative, Quality of probable reasoning; because the differences of the one are determinate, of the other indeterminate.

Quantity is particularly interesting and important, as forming the subject of the only perfect science we possess—Mathematics. From what has been above said, it follows that if pure Mathematics be really the science of Quantity, as is universally allowed, then that science is altogether independent of Matter. The definitions of Euclid prove the same thing. A point, we are told, is that which has position, but not magnitude. A line is length without breadth. But in the material world there are no such points and lines; therefore pure Geometry is not a science of Matter. Is it, then, a branch of Mental Science? Certainly not, in the general acceptation of that term; for Quantity has nothing to do with Mind or Spirit, either with the Substance thereof or the phenomena. Who ever heard of half a soul, or of two-thirds of a sensation, thought, or emotion? But if pure Mathematics be neither a material nor a mental science, what can it be? for that division seems to exhaust the subject. We answer that it is the science of Quantity, under its three modifications of Space, Time, and Number. Arithmetic is the Science of Number; Geometry, of Extension, whether of one, two, or three dimensions; while Algebra comprehends Number, Extension, and Time; for letters may apply to any of these. Such is pure Mathematics; which ought to be classed apart, in a comprehensive division of the sciences, and not to be confounded either with mental or with material or physical science, with which last it is commonly joined. It is a science strictly *sui generis*, or a *summum genus*, embracing three species, Arithmetic, Geometry, and Algebra. According to this view, science would embrace three leading divisions, Metaphysics, Physics, and Mathematics.[b]

Belonging to this subject there is a very interesting question, as to the foundation and nature of Mathematical certainty. Since that science treats neither of Mind nor of Matter, it follows that its certainty depends not upon the existence of either of these. Let the earth be dissolved, and all that live thereon, still the truths of Mathematics will remain. Whatever exists as Matter or as Mind may change, or cease to be, and therefore the science thereof may fail; but we must alter or set bounds to time and space before we can change the certainty of Mathematics.

It has been said by an exceedingly able writer of the present day, (See *Mill's System of Logic*, Book ii. chap. v.) that the certainty of Mathematics is merely hypothetical; that its propositions are true in the sense that they follow irresistibly from an hypothesis, and in that sense only. Thus, when a line is defined as length without breadth, or a triangle as a figure with three sides and three angles, we are told that the tacit assumption is made, " and such a thing exists." On this assumption, and others similar, it is said, rest all the demonstrations of Mathematics. When we define a line as above, do we then really mean to imply that such a line exists in the world of matter?

If we do, then we enounce, at the very beginning, a notorious falsehood; and no conclusions drawn from it can be worth attending to. The boasted science of Mathematics becomes like the ravings of a madman, who first fancies himself a king, and then reasons well accordingly.

But if what we have above said, as to the nature of Quantity, be correct, then Mathematical demonstration is quite independent of Matter; and consequently we do not assume that the points, lines, triangles, circles, &c. as defined in books of Geometry, have any existence in the material universe. No doubt it was by the material world that we first became acquainted with points, lines, triangles, &c. approximating to those defined; but having once got these ideas, through our sensations, we can afterwards detach them from Matter, and consider them as modifications of pure space. Look at the arch of a bridge. Without the stone and lime which form the arch I might never have conceived a curve; but, having once seen a curve in Matter, I can imagine one immaterial. What is included between the arch, the piers, and the water below, forms a definite figure in empty space, the air being invisible. From constant association with Matter it is, no doubt, difficult, if not impossible, to avoid thinking of Matter when we wish to think of figure only, and sensible diagrams are even put before us; but in framing or following the reasoning, we can attend so little to what is material, as not to be at all disturbed thereby in our calculations. I have, then, a notion of a Mathematical line, triangle, circle, &c., and a notion sufficiently clear to conduct me through the longest chain of reasoning without any confusion; and what more can I wish?

But, if such points, lines, and circles, &c., exist not in any material object, and if spirit be altogether inconsistent with extension and figure, can these points, lines, and circles, be said to exist at all? and if not, is the science purely imaginary? The only answer to this is, that if space can be said to exist, then do the figures of Geometry. They rest upon the same foundation, they must stand or fall together; and if Space and Time be not imaginary, neither is the science of Mathematics. Surely no one will say that the terms, Space and Time, have either no meaning at all, or mean what exists only in fancy, as the words Centaur, Mermaid. The same exactly may be said of the lines and figures of Geometry. That these terms have a meaning is evident, for otherwise how could we reason about them? and if they have a meaning, then we have notions corresponding to them, for these are but different phrases for the same thing. And will any one pretend that those notions are fanciful, like the notions of Centaur and Mermaid? We have then notions, and notions which are not fantastic, what more can we desire for Truth?

With all respect for the abilities of the abovementioned author, I cannot but think that his doctrine, with respect to necessary truths, is fundamentally erroneous. Certain it is that philosophers have long made a distinction between necessary and contingent truth, a distinction which Mr. Mill would confound. Hume clearly marked out the difference, under the names of relations of ideas, and matters of fact, the latter known by experience, the former not. Dr. Whewell's account of this, as quoted by Mr. Mill, is as follows: "Necessary truths are those in which we not only learn that the proposition *is* true, but see that it *must* be true; in which the negative of the truth is not only false but impossible, in which we cannot, even by an effort of imagination, or in a supposition, conceive the reverse of that which is asserted. That there are such truths cannot be doubted. We may take for example all relations of number. Three and two, added together, make five; we cannot conceive it to be otherwise; we cannot by any freak of thought imagine three and two to make seven."[c]

From this passage Mr. Mill deduces that, according to Dr. Whewell, a necessary truth may be defined to be a proposition, the negative of which is not only false, but inconceivable. Starting from this idea, Mr. Mill goes on to show that as the power of conception depends very much upon association, and as many things formerly supposed inconceivable, are now not only conceived but believed; for instance, the action of bodies on each other at a distance; of Matter on Mind, &c., he thence infers that inconceivability of the contrary is a very poor test of truth, and that what is called necessary truth rests, like every other, solely on experience.

Is there then no difference in the evidence on which these two propositions rest? The sun will rise to-morrow; the three angles of a triangle are equal to two right angles. Are they both contingent, or both necessary? Do they both rest upon experience? Consult your own mind. Why do we believe that the sun will rise to-morrow? Because as far as I know personally, or can learn from the testimony of others, alive or dead, it always has in time past. But can you see in that any irresistible reason why it should rise to-

[c] Philosophy of the Inductive Sciences, Part i. Book i. Chap. 9.

morrow? Must you not allow, that, for aught you know, the sun may be dissolved, and scattered throughout boundless space before another day? Ere you can say positively *it will not*, your knowledge must be far far more extended than it is at present, it must approximate to the knowledge of *Him* who created the sun and all things. But why do you believe that the three angles of a triangle are equal to two right angles? Because I have seen it demonstrated; that is, starting from some self-evident truth, I have followed a chain of reasoning, each link of which was an irresistible inference from the preceding, until I arrived at the conclusion, which was the last irresistible inference. The demonstration finished, I can no more doubt the truth in question, than I can doubt the existence of that feeling of which at the moment I am conscious. I see clearly that the conclusion holds good, and always will hold good; in short, that it *must* be true.

But how do you know that? All I can answer is that I see it to be so. I assert that to me the first proposition is self-evident, and that the inferences flow from it irresistibly, even to the conclusion. If you deny this, I can only bid you to study the theorem. Should you still persist in your doubts I can say no more, for I cannot give a demonstration of a demonstration. What is self-evident not only requires no proof, but admits of none; and if the inferences from the first proposition be not directly felt to be irresistible, no arguments remain to make them so.

Having read and mentally followed the theorem in which the above conclusion is established, *can* any man doubt its truth? If he cannot, then the truth is necessary, not contingent. And if he cannot doubt its truth, then is it not derived from experience; for experience tells us only of the past; and we can always doubt whether what we have experienced in the past shall happen again.

If this be correct, it is absurd to ask for any test of self-evidence, or of demonstrative inference. You either see it, or you do not. A necessary truth is that which is either evident at once, or becomes so by means of a demonstration. The criterion is not that the opposite is a contradiction in terms, for I see no contradiction in supposing, previous to enquiry, that the three angles of a triangle are greater or less than two right angles; no contradiction to the definition of triangle. It is not as if I said that black is white. Neither is inconceivability of the contrary a criterion; for, beforehand, I can just as well conceive that those three angles are unequal as equal to two right angles. But Dr. Whewell having made use of the word *conceive*, Mr. Mill has founded thereon a supposed refutation of the doctrine that there are truths, necessary truths, which we know for certain, but not from experience. No doubt when truths are seen to be necessary, the contrary is inconceivable; but it is not because they may be inconceivable that we deem them necessary.

When we say that a truth is necessary, we imply that the contrary is impossible, the one involves the other; and if we require a criterion of necessity, so do we of impossibility. But neither admits of any that can be stated in words: the mind alone supplies it.

The distinctions between Quantity and Quality may be here summed up.

1. Quality varies by insensible shades or degrees; whereas one Quantity differs from another by a fixed or determinate difference.

2. Quality generally, but not always, admits of a contrary, as black is the contrary of white, wetness of dryness, hardness of softness, vice of virtue, ugliness of beauty: but Quantity has never a contrary. One Quantity may be double, triple, four times, another quantity; but in all these there is no opposition; but only more or less of the same thing.

3. Qualities are like or unlike; but Quanti-

ties are equal or unequal. This last distinction, however, is comprehended under the first; for where the degrees of difference are insensible, there will be likeness or unlikeness; and where the differences are fixed, there will be equality or inequality.

# RELATION.

In treating of Quality we have been led, unavoidably, to mention RELATION; but this word now demands a separate head.

In classifying the phenomena of Mind, Relations are opposed to Conceptions, and they are thus distinguished: Conceptions being those inward phenomena which do not necessarily imply, or at least do not evidently imply, the existence of two things; while Relations do manifestly suppose more things than one. I look at a horse present before me, and admire his form, colour, and activity, without thinking of any other horse; and I have a Perception of him, which, in his absence, may suggest a Conception. I consider him along with a pony, and I compare them; in other words, I am conscious of a Relation between them. And this state of mind which I experience is quite distinct from the Perception or the Conception, either of the horse or of the pony; though but for those, it never would have arisen. It is a state more removed from Sensation, in the order of time, than either Perception or Conception, of which it is the consequence.

So far the distinction between Conception and Relation seems very clearly marked; though when we examine the matter more deeply we shall find that there are but very few conceptions which do not at least imply, that is suppose in a covert way, the existence of more things than one. Thus, all the qualities of Substances, even those which we have called Simple, as opposed to Relative, suppose not only that there is an outward or material object, but also a percipient mind. A blue object is one which rouses in me the sensation which I call blueness, and therefore there is a relation between that object and myself. Still, there is a difference between this case and that of a Relation, commonly so called; a difference on which we have enlarged, in treating of Quality. Besides the more complex nature of the Relation in the latter case, it is also manifestly *felt*; whereas in the former, it is discovered only by those who study the subject metaphysically. No one, generally speaking, when looking at a green field, thinks of the field, then of his sensation, and lastly of the Relation between them. It would be a bad use of metaphysical subtlety to confound distinctions recognized by the common sense, as well as the common language, of all mankind. The words blueness, redness, hardness, softness, wetness, dryness, suggest no Relation to ordinary men; but those of father, mother, brother, sister, cousin, tutor, governor, servant, slave, cannot be heard by any one without calling up the notion of two persons somehow connected. A Relation, then, considered as a mental phenomenon, is an inward state of mind, which manifestly supposes the existence of two things at least, having something in common; and according to the nature of that something, there are different kinds of Relations.

But do Relations exist only as mental phenomena? Have they no existence outwardly?

Objects there are, we allow, having an independent existence without; but it would be palpable nonsense to say that a Relation exists as Matter exists. That it is, however, something more than a mere state of mind, every one is convinced. When I think of a mare and her foal, I am conscious that there exists a connection between them, (the nature of which every dolt knows as well as the wisest of men), consisting of a long series of material changes in which the two participate; but if you ask me to put my finger on the Relation as on a lump of Matter, then I am quite at a loss. I must allow that the Relation exists not as the mare and her foal exist—objects which can be seen and touched. Must

I then be driven to confess that the Relation between them is a mere state of my Mind? But this conclusion is as opposed to the universal sense of mankind as the other. How then can the Relation exist if it be neither material merely nor mental merely? This is a question which I will answer when any one shall inform me how Space and Time exist.

Having explained, as far as we are able, the nature of Relation, let us see what are the different kinds thereof.

There is one distinction among Relations which is very well marked. Some Relations suppose the things related to exist simultaneously or together; others imply that they exist in succession: consequently the latter do, and the former do not, necessarily involve the notion of time. We have, therefore, Relations of co-existence, and Relations of succession; these always supposing time, while those may or may not suppose space, according as the objects related are outward and material, or inward and mental. The following are the principal relations of co-existence.

1. Relations of Position. I stand on a mountain commanding an extensive prospect. I descry hills, dales, woods, towers, steeples; I remark how they lie one with another, east, west, north, or south; some nearer, some farther off; some

above, some below; and I am conscious that they are related in space, related by position. This relation is the foundation or subject of Geography and descriptive Astronomy; of Zoology, so far as the mere collocation of parts, as known by Anatomy, is concerned; of Botany also to a considerable extent; and of Geology likewise in part, one object of which is to determine the relative position of strata.

2. Relations of Comprehension. I look down from the top of St. Paul's, and I see a vast city, which in a certain sense I consider one, but which embraces or contains within it an immense number of streets, squares, houses, churches, &c., and I am conscious of a relation between the whole and the parts, between things existing in space, a Relation of Comprehension. This is the subject of all those sciences which are properly called analytic, or which investigate the constitution of things, such as Analytic Chymistry, which searches after the hidden ingredients of material objects, and Analytic Metaphysics; though in this case the things related, viz., the compound feeling, and the simple feelings which it comprises, cannot be said to have any existence in space.

3. Relations of Quantity. Quantity being, as we have seen, that which hath parts, and which may be increased or diminished without limit, by

adding or subtracting parts, it would seem to follow that, as in this sense, both time and space have Quantity, therefore the Relations of Quantity ought to be classed, some as co-existing, others as successive. But in reality it is not so. As for the theorems of pure Geometry, these are evidently concerned with the Relations of things in space, for they may be represented to the eye, though with some imperfection. And though the numbers of Arithmetic and the letters of Algebra may apply to the divisions of time as well as of space, yet while making our calculations, while feeling the Relations in question, the Quantities are supposed to co-exist. While we are conscious that 2 : 4 : : 4 : 8, all these numbers exist together; and though we may afterwards insert the word *hours*, and say that 2 hours : 4 hours : : 4 hours : 8 hours, yet this insertion cannot change the nature of a Relation previously felt.

Relations of Quantity, then, and the science of those Relations, viz., pure Mathematics, do not, in any case, involve the notion of Time.[d]

---

[d] Since writing the above, I am glad to find my opinion confirmed by that of Mr. Mill. "The laws of number," says he, "are common to synchronous and successive phenomena." Again, "the laws of number, though true of successive phenomena, do not relate to their succession."—See Mill's System of Logic, Book iii. Chap. 5.

4. *Relations of Indeterminate degree.* I look upon two tulips, and pronounce one to be more gaudy than another; upon two geraniums, and perceive that the one has the more brilliant colours; upon two horses, a racer and a cart horse, and am conscious that the former is the more finely formed; upon two women, and am sensible that the one is much more beautiful than the other.

So, I partake of two loaves of bread, and am aware that they are of different degrees of goodness, or of different qualities, as the phrase is.

All these are Relations of Indeterminate degree; for by what standard can we measure them? We may be sure that one thing surpasses another in brilliancy of colour, in beauty, in taste, or in nutritive power, but who can say how much? The qualities or properties compared must, of course, be similar, for between different qualities, as between colour and taste, beauty and nutritive power, there can be no comparison. True it is that the word *Quality* is sometimes used to signify *degree,* as when we speak of different qualities of bread or meat, meaning different degrees of goodness, as to taste and nutrition; and in this sense diverse qualities or degrees may be compared; but this is a popular, not a philosophical sense of the word. And as

F

the word *degree* is often used to express Relations of Quantity, as in the case of the degrees of a thermometer, therefore it is necessary to distinguish the Relation now in question by the phrase *Indeterminate degree.*

In popular language the word *Quality*, in the sense of *Degree*, is very commonly opposed to *Quantity;* as when we say that the food of the poor is both deficient in Quantity, and bad in Quality; that is, inferior either in taste or in nutritive power to the food consumed by the rich. But we must be careful not to confound this sense of the word Quality with the philosophical one. In the philosophical sense, different Qualities or Properties, as Taste, and Nutritive Power, cannot be compared together; but in the popular sense different Qualities may be compared, because Quality then signifies degree of a common Property; as the degree of excellence in food as to the common Property Taste, or else as to Nutritive Power.

Here we again see the difference between Quality in the strict or philosophical sense, and Quantity; the former admitting of Relations of Indeterminate degree, and of those only; the latter of Relations only of determinate degree. This distinction is of the utmost importance, as it at once separates Mathematics, or the Science of Quantity, as susceptible of demonstration and certainty, from all other Sciences, which admit only of probability.

Some Qualities are much more determinate than others. Thus Justice is much more so than any other duty; and consequently, the Science of Law is the most exact department of Moral Philosophy.

These four are perhaps the only orders of Relations which are always between things co-existent. The second class, or Relations of Succession, is divided into two orders, according as the sequence is invariable or casual. The former is the important relation of Cause and Effect, which will be treated at length by and by.

How important to Philosophy is a right notion of Cause and Effect, may be judged from the fact that this is the object of Philosophy properly so called, as distinguished from simple Science. And what wandering in the dark do we find among philosophers from not knowing what they were seeking! To trace the sequences of Cause and Effect is one object, but to mount up to General Causes or Principles is the highest scope of philosophy. The whole is comprised in two words—Causation and Generalization.

The second order of successive Relations is that of casual succession, one of little importance, because, as the name implies, it cannot be calculated or foretold.

But though not important in itself, it has nevertheless been the occasion of most of the errors in philosophy as well as in daily life. As I have elsewhere observed, so great is the tendency to connect things as Cause and Effect, that with children, and ignorant adults, one instance of sequence is enough to create the belief of invariability; and nothing but a wider experience can correct this tendency. There is perhaps not a man, however experienced, who does not still make such mistakes; though certainly he will not believe that Tenterden Church Steeple was the cause of the Goodwin sands, because it was built just before their appearance. We must not confound casual succession with accident, for the latter implies a real sequence of Cause and Effect, but one which could not have been foretold, owing to the great complication of causes in the world, and our ignorance of most of them; whereas in Casual Succession there is no connection of the kind between the two events, no more than between Tenterden and Goodwin. The one simply precedes, and the other follows, on a single occasion, and that is all; and ten thousand things, as well as the one in question, may have preceded the latter. How many events must have immediately gone before my act of writing these lines on paper!

Besides these two classes of Relations, the co-existent and the successive, there seems to be a third class, comprising Relations, some of which are co-existent and others successive. This may be called the mixed class. To it belongs but one order, exceedingly comprehensive, the Relations of Resemblance.

Resemblance may be felt either between things co-existent, as between two horses, or two sheep, placed side by side, or between two sequences of phenomena; as when two billiard balls are each impelled by another; or as when two salts are produced, in the one case by mixing sulphuric acid with potash, in another muriatic acid with soda. Here not only the products of the chemical action are alike in some important particulars, but the actions themselves are very similar. So we say that there is a striking resemblance between the revolutionary changes which took place in England, in the seventeenth century, and those which occurred in France, in the eighteenth and nineteenth; meaning not only that the results were alike, but that the events succeeded each other in a like order.

No Relation is more generally felt than that of Resemblance. Though we frequently say of two things, that they are not the least alike, yet this is only in comparison with others that are more like; for, strictly speaking, almost all things have something in common; some one point, at least, of resemblance.

To determine important Resemblances is one grand object of Science. All classification is founded on Resemblance, and in many Sciences classification is everything. When we shall have classified all the objects of the animal, vegetable, and mineral kingdoms, according to their resemblances, descriptive natural history will be complete. In Mental Science also classification of the phenomena of mind is an important part. But more than this, all our reasonings from experience, all induction, as it is commonly called, is founded on this same relation; for the fundamental axiom of inductive reasoning is that nature is uniform in her operations; that like causes will be followed by like effects, and that things which have constantly co-existed, will always co-exist; for instance, that a creature having the outward appearance of a man, will always have a heart, liver, lungs, &c., formed like other men, whom we have actually examined. The grand object of inquiry then, becomes, to detect in any new case sufficient similarity with an old case, that is sufficient to warrant us in inferring similar co-existence of things, or similar succession of phenomena, without actual observation. Resemblance, then, and Causation are Relations of the utmost importance in Science and Philosophy.

It seems scarcely necessary to add that the study of Resemblances belongs as well to the Poet as to the Philosopher. How much of the charm of the fine arts depends upon the likeness between their creations and those of nature! And are not the finest parts of poetry the similes? For the sake of beauty, a simile must be neither very near nor very far fetched; for in the one case it is indifferent, in the other ludicrous. A simile scientifically correct would be about as bad in poetry as one that is absurd.[e]

[e] Relations of Resemblance may be considered either as a class distinct from those of co-existence, and those of sucession, or the Resemblances of co-existence may be looked upon as an order of the former class, and resemblances of succession as an order of the latter. This however would be not at all a logical arrangement, for then we should separate the species of the genus resemblance, and place them under different classes.

## POWER, CAUSE AND EFFECT.

Though we have made mention of Cause and Effect under the head of Relation, yet, as this is the most important of all relations, and probably the least understood, it seems necessary to consider it now at large under a separate head.

Power is the word which expresses that peculiar relation which a Cause bears to its Effect, the nature of which we are now to investigate. What then is the notion which we actually have of Power?

In the first place it is evident that by Cause we mean something which precedes something else, which something else we call Effect. The relation between them then, or Power, is a relation of antecedence and consequence, in other words, of Succession, involving the notion of Time; and the order of this succession is uniform, the Cause being the antecedent, the Effect always the consequent. But ten thousand things may precede any change, only one of which we look upon as the Cause of that change. Therefore, a Cause is not a mere antecedent; an Effect not a mere consequent

When we have determined the cause of any phenomenon, we believe that it will be followed by that effect, not only once, not only several times, not only most times, but always; and if perchance we be deceived, and at any time the cause appear without the effect, we draw one or the other of the following conclusions. Either we were altogether wrong in the supposed cause, or the one now before us differs in some respect from that which we formerly observed; or, what is nearly the same thing, there are other counteracting causes at work which we wot not of. But, however we may account for the failure of the effect, we never for a moment suppose that there is any want of uniformity in Nature, or that causes really alike in all respects will not always be followed by like Effects. A man who should hazard such an opinion would be considered out of his mind. So far then we tread upon indisputable ground; and we can pronounce, without doubt, that Power involves the notion of Invariable Antecedence and Invariable Consequence.

But is this the whole of the Relation, as some philosophers assert, particularly Thomas Brown? That acute metaphysician, treading in the steps of Hume, wrote a book to prove that all we know, or ever can know, of Cause and Effect, is, that the one invariably precedes, the other invariably follows. Events, as Hume observed, are conjoined, but as far as we can trace, unconnected. Nothing seems to bind them together. They succeed each other, some invariably, others casually, but we never can say why any order prevails, why fire warms or cold freezes, why acids and alkalis combine to form salts. Pursue your investigation as far as you can, says Brown, try and find out some connection between any cause and its effect, and if you seem to succeed, what will you have learnt? Simply this: that between the two there is a link, (if we may so call it), formerly unknown, a change previously undiscovered; so that instead of A followed immediately by C, we have A followed by B, followed by C, a sequence more full, but merely a sequence, and quite as incomprehensible as before. The only difference is, that A is no longer considered the Invariable and Immediate Antecedent of C, but simply an Invariable Antecedent, while it is the Immediate and Invariable Antecedent of B.

This doctrine may be true, but it must be allowed that it sounds strange in the ears of untutored men, and at first, at least, appears unsatisfactory to all. That a Cause is something more than an Invariable Antecedent, an Effect than an Invariable Consequent, we cannot help believing, though what it can be may transcend our limited intelligence. But if the above be the only definite notion of Power which we possess, we ought not to find fault with the doctrine because it openly acknowledges our ignorance. Is it however certain that we have no other notion of Power? The general sense of mankind would induce us to think that we have, for those who cannot refute the above doctrine are still unsatisfied, and though silenced, are not convinced. But where interest or passion does not intervene, truth, though long undiscovered, when once pointed out is apt to seize upon the mind with the force of intuition. This is particularly the case with metaphysical truth, which is known to us ultimately by consciousness. To the mind of each individual must we appeal, as to the highest tribunal, in all questions relative to mental philosophy; and this tribunal seems to decide that the above doctrine of Cause and Effect is not altogether satisfactory.

This general consideration may make us suspect the doctrine of Brown, but, to refute it, some definite objection is necessary. And this objection has been furnished by Reid, who remarks that if a Cause be merely an Invariable Antecedent, an Effect an Invariable Consequent, then, as no two events have more constantly succeeded each other than day and night, night and day, it will follow that day is the Cause of the succeeding night, night the Cause of the succeeding day. Nor does it seem easy to answer this objection. It is quite conceivable that a common cause, or union of causes, as in this case the existence and fixity of the sun, combined with the rotation of the earth, may give rise to a series of changes, succeeding each other invariably, though unconnected as Cause and Effect. The very power of conceiving such an occurrence proves that there is no inconsistency in the notion of invariable succession without causation, and here we produce a case where such a succession actually takes place. We must then conclude that the doctrine of Hume and Brown, as to Cause and Effect, is, to say the least, incomplete. That invariable antecedence belongs to a Cause, invariable consequence to an Effect, is undoubtedly true; but it is not the whole truth.

Mankind seem to be generally convinced that there is what they call a *necessary connection* between Cause and Effect. But what is meant by this phrase? The only sense which I can here attach to the word *necessary* is that of *indispensable*. When we say that the truths of Mathematics are necessary, we mean either that they are self-evident, or that they follow irresistibly by reasoning from self-evident truths. This necessity the mind sees intimately; it sees that the truths are not contingent, not liable to change now or hereafter; unchangeable even by omnipotence. The same can be said of no matters of fact. The world and all that it inherits may change in the twinkling of an eye, *for aught that we can see to the contrary*, and, therefore, in this sense of necessity we can see no necessary connection between any two successive events. This, however, we do find out by experience, that in the present state of existence, at any rate, and until some grand change shall ensue, certain events are indispensable to certain others; in other words, unless the former occur, the latter will not follow. The one we call Cause, the other Effect; and we say that the one has Power to produce the other, meaning that it is an indispensable condition of its existence. A Cause, then, is not a mere invariable antecedent, but it is an invariable and indispensable antecedent; and as the word *Indispensable* evidently includes invariability and something more, the word *Invariable* becomes unnecessary; and we may define a Cause to be *an Indispensable Antecedent*, an Effect, *an Unavoidable Consequent*.

Having determined the nature of Cause and

Effect in general, that is to say the general notion which we have of the relation between them, it remains to be seen whether Causes may not be divided into different species. Aristotle mentions four kinds of Causes—the Material, the Formal, the Efficient, and the Final; but we need not long be detained with these, for most of them would not now be regarded as Causes at all.[f]

What he calls the Material Cause, is the substance of which a thing is made, as the material cause of a silver spoon, is the metal silver; and if the substance be a compound one, as brass, then the material causes thereof are the simple bodies or elements, in this case copper and zinc. This, then, is not a cause in our sense of the word. Again, the Formal Cause, as the ancients understood it, is purely imaginary; and the Final Cause is properly not a cause, but an effect which we see, an useful effect, the foresight of which, as we presume, induced the Great Creator to provide means suitable to the end in view. It is only as offering a motive to the mind of the Deity that an end in view, an effect anticipated, becomes a Cause. Of the four Causes of Aristotle

---

[f] These four Causes were very neatly expressed in Greek, by four prepositions. The Material Cause was the ἐξ οὗ (out of which); the Formal, the καθ ὅ' (according to which); the Efficient, the ὑφ'οῦ (by which); and the Final, the διὰ ὅ' (for which.)

there remains then only the Efficient which we should recognise as such; the principle of motion, the indispensable antecedent of any change.

The first and most obvious division of causes, is that into Immediate and Remote. Since causes form a lengthened chain, reaching from visible effects up to the great First Cause, it follows that some are nearer to the effect, others farther off. Properly speaking there is but one immediate cause, and all the others are remote, though in different degrees.

Often do two men differ as to the causes of any phenomenon, but both may be right; for the cause hit upon by the one may be more remote than that assigned by the other, and each may exist in its order. Thus, while some maintain that value and price are regulated by the demand and supply, others insist that cost of production is the determining cause. Nor is there here any real opposition, for cost of production regulates the demand and supply, and these again regulate price.

Causes are also divided into Proximate and Ultimate. Judging by Etymology or the derivation of the words, we might suppose that Proximate and Ultimate mean exactly the same thing as Immediate and Remote; and such is the uncertainty in the use of words that we cannot affirm that they never are so employed; but generally speaking the sense is very different. For *Immediate* and *Remote* refer to the real order of succession of phenomena in causation, (one after another), whereas *Proximate* and *Ultimate* relate to the order according to which we arrive at the knowledge of causes. Thus Proximate corresponds to palpable or apparent; Ultimate, to hidden or real. For the real causes of change are not always manifest, often far otherwise, being enveloped, and so hidden from view, by masses of inert matter. As a remedy for ague the value of bark was known for ages, but of late years only has it been discovered that the whole virtue resides in a very small portion of the mass, in a substance that can be separated from the rest, and which is called *Quinine*. So the whole narcotic virtue of opium has been found to reside in *Morphia*, and the poisoning property of nux vomica in the alkali *Strycknia*: and bark, opium, and the nux vomica, are the Proximate or palpable causes; quinine, morphia, and strycknia, the Ultimate, hidden, or real causes.

Proximate and Ultimate, then, refer not to the order of succession among the phenomena of causation, but to the order in which we discover them. The compound substance bark is not nearer in time to the effect, viz. the cure of ague, than is the simpler substance quinine; but the whole effect, as we find by experience, is owing to the latter, and the former deprived of this contributes nothing. If anything, the woody matter rather hinders than promotes the good result. Bark is indeed still a cure for ague; but it is so only because it contains the alkali Quinine. The rest is merely the covering of the real cause, the garment which conceals it from view.

The grand object of philosophy, mental or physical, is to trace ultimate causes, to ascend to them, as the phrase is, from the proximate and palpable causes which lie upon the flat before us. It is therefore of the utmost consequence clearly to understand their nature. This, it is hoped, will in part appear from the above remarks. The examples derived from chemistry are particularly valuable as illustrations, because the proximate and ultimate causes of change can there be actually exhibited as substances. But it is not so in all sciences. Very frequently the ultimate causes of change are not substances but *tendencies;* tendencies inseparable from mind or matter, but not to be seen or felt, and known only from the result. Thus we attribute the motion of the earth round the sun to two *Tendencies* at present supposed ultimate, a projectile rectilinear, or tangential force, and the force of gravity. These tendencies being given, we can from their union account for the motion of the earth as their common result; though the latter only is strictly proved, the former being only hypothetical.

Whatever may be the point which we have reached in the progress of our enquiry, whether the causes already discovered be the most general and simple that can be traced by man or not, for the time at least they are ultimate causes; like those fifty or sixty bodies which chemists call simple, because they have never been analyzed. But is it not often said that man can discover proximate causes only, ultimate being beyond his ken? When this is asserted, it must mean that the Deity is not only the great first, the original or remote cause of the phenomena of the universe, but also the real or ultimate cause of every event; that nothing takes place, not only without his permission, but without his direct agency.

This may be the case, and it may be that God is thus the one ultimate or real cause of every change, but the question is clearly beyond the sphere of human intellect; and whatever opinion we may adopt on this point, we are justified in distinguishing between those causes which lie more open to view, and those more hidden; and, speaking comparatively, we may call the former proximate, the latter ultimate, though these may not be strictly such, not ultimate even to our limited capabilities, but so only provisionally.

The words Proximate and Ultimate, as here explained, exactly correspond in meaning with the use of them in analytic chemistry. What are called the proximate principles of any compound are those constituent parts which meet us first in the order of analysis, they being themselves compounded of the ultimate principles or elements, and much more like to the compound than are those elements. Thus the proximate principles of animal substances—of muscle, cellular tissue, serous membranes, nerves, blood, lymph, &c., are found to be fibrin, gelatin, gluten, &c., all which principles are made up chiefly, if not entirely, of four elements—Carbon, Oxygen, Hydrogen, and Nitrogen or Azote, in different proportions.

Another division of Causes is that into Primary and Secondary. As immediate and remote relate to the real order of succession, and proximate and ultimate to the natural order of discovery, so primary and secondary refer to the order of importance. Since few, if any events, are owing to one cause alone, a distinction is made according to the degree in which causes are supposed to contribute towards the common result, and one is called Primary, while others are styled Secondary or Auxiliary. In this sense Gibbon professedly uses the term *Secondary* in his celebrated chapter on the Propagation of Christianity; though the writer insidiously endeavours to instil into his readers that his five causes were sufficient to account for the marvellous effect, that in short they were primary, not secondary causes. Since secondary causes are often subsequent in the order of time to the primary, they may be at once auxiliary and immediate, and the word secondary may be sometimes used in one sense, sometimes in the other; being now opposed to primary or principal, now to remote or original. Thus, when we talk of the secondary causes of moral sentiment, we may mean to distinguish them from primary, in the sense of original, or in the sense of principal or chief; and as the same causes which are secondary in the one sense are so likewise in the other, neither the reader nor the writer may be always aware in which sense the word is used. The Original Causes of moral sentiment, which are also the most important, are certain tendencies deeply and indelibly seated in the human mind; whereas the secondary or subsequent causes, which are likewise of less consequence, are such fluctuating circumstances as Education, Passion, Local Utility, &c. The word *Circumstance* is commonly used to express a secondary or auxiliary cause, which, along with others of the same sort, is supposed, as it were, to stand around the primary or principal cause.

What is called an OCCASION is nothing but a secondary or auxiliary cause. Thus, I say that it was on occasion of my being in London that I went to see the British Museum; meaning that this circumstance went along with the principal cause, which undoubtedly was my desire to see the curiosities therein contained. But had this desire been very strong, I might have gone up to London on purpose. So we pray against all " occasions of evil;" that is, all outward circumstances which may help to stir up the great source of mischief—our own bad propensities.

An OPPORTUNITY is also an auxiliary cause, one that facilitates the acquisition of any object which we are supposed to have previously desired. The keener the desire, the quicker generally is the intellect in seeing opportunities, and the greater the readiness in seizing upon them. The grand art of life is that of perceiving and profiting by opportunities. "Ideas come again, convictions perpetuate themselves, opportunities never recur."

There is another distinction which deserves to be mentioned; one dwelt upon chiefly by medical writers, viz., the division of causes into Predisponent and Exciting.

Two men go out together and are exposed to the same weather; with the same precautions, or want of precautions, both get wet to the skin, return home, and both immediately change, or not, as the case may be; but the one catches only a slight cold, and the other falls ill and dies of consumption. Here medical men would say that the one had the seeds of consumption undeveloped in his frame, before he was exposed to the exciting causes of cold and wet, the other not; or that the former was predisposed to that fatal malady. And assuredly there are great diversities of constitution—original tendencies to different diseases in different persons, or we never could account for the diverse effects of the same outward causes. But those tendencies may be long hidden, or even may never be known, in the absence of any outward or exciting cause; as a consumptive habit may never actually fall into consumption, if fatigue, cold, and wet, be carefully avoided. Therefore the division of causes into Predisposing and Exciting is not only very useful, as a guide to the medical practitioner, but it may lay claim to no small degree of philosophical accuracy.

# LAW.

WHAT is a Law?

A Law, in its most general sense, means *a General Rule, proceeding from an intelligent being.* Now Laws are of two sorts—Speculative and Practical. Speculative Laws, often called the Laws of Nature, are those general rules or plans which we suppose to have been present to the mind of the Deity, or great First Cause, before he formed the universe, and according to which he afterwards did form the same. To us, these laws are in the first instance merely an object of speculation; though the knowledge of them may subsequently be turned to the most important practical purposes. To discover these laws is the grand object of Natural and Mental Philosophy.

When we talk of the laws which govern the universe, or any department of the universe, we must remember that though in one point of view these laws are causes, yet in another they are themselves effects, and therefore requiring explanation quite as much as the phenomena which they help to explain. Therefore these laws only remove the difficulty a few steps, and to a great self-existent cause we must have recourse at last. Laws then, after all, are but God's deputies; and their government is only delegated.[g]

A Practical Law, on the other hand, is a general rule proceeding from an intelligent being or beings, whereby something is commanded to be done, or not to be done, under the sanction of reward or punishment. This law may be written or unwritten, expressed or understood, partial or universal, temporary or eternal. Practical Laws are also divided into the Ethical and the Political.

In an Ethical Law, or as some call it, a Natural Law, (because the knowledge of it is obtained by the use of natural, *i. e.* our common or ordinary faculties, without any peculiar study), the rule is supposed to proceed from all men, or what comes to the same thing, from God; for whatever is held by all men, at all times, must be derived from unchangeable principles of human nature, which we must suppose implanted in us on purpose by Him. The rule, then, which here is a command, proceeds from all men, or from God, and the sanction is fear of punishment, or hope of reward, from man or from God; from man individually, not from men united in a body politic or commonwealth. The principal sanction of man individually is approbation or disapprobation, moral love, or moral indignation, and their consequences.

[g] For a further account of Law of Nature see next article.

These Laws may admit of some modifications, according to times and circumstances, but no further than the nature of man himself for whose use they are framed, is liable to change. As compared with those which follow, they may therefore be called immutable and eternal.

A Political law is a general rule, whereby the sovereign of a state or commonwealth commands or forbids something, under the sanction of reward or punishment. Laws of this sort may vary very widely according to the will of the sovereign, either in the same country at different times, or in different countries at the same time; though it follows directly from what is above said, that a Political ought never to be contrary to an Ethical Law.[h]

---

[h] The term Political, as here used, means the law of the State in general, and comprises, not only constitutional or organic law, but the criminal, as well as what is particularly called the civil law. All laws, in short, made by the governing power of a State, I call *Political.*

# LAW OF NATURE.

## EXPLANATION OF PHENOMENA.

Few phrases are more used in Philosophy, and few are more imperfectly comprehended than LAW OF NATURE. This then requires a separate article.

A Law of Nature may be defined to be *a General Effect, or Tendency to an Effect, of which the Cause is unknown.*

From this it follows that a Law cannot be explained; it can only be stated, not accounted for. But this general effect or tendency must in the course of nature be a cause of other phenomena; and consequently, though itself unaccountable, it may serve to explain other things.

There is then no absurdity in assigning a Law in explanation of any Phenomenon; for though in one view it is an effect inexplicable, in another it is a cause. Nay, a law is the ultimate explanation of any phenomenon, in other words, the ultimate cause, so far as we know, the most simple and general that can be pointed out by us; always excepting the first Great Cause of all, which alone is really ultimate. Once more, to explain a phenomenon is to assign the cause thereof. But the cause first observed may be only proximate or palpable, containing the simple and general, or real cause, along with other things of no moment; and when we have separated these last we have detached the ultimate cause, which, if it be a tendency and not a substance, is called a law of nature. Therefore, in this sense of the word Law, explanation by assigning a cause, and explanation by pointing out a law, are not different in kind, and not opposed; but explanation by cause comprehends two species, explanation by proximate causes, and explanation by ultimate causes or laws.

A complex effect may be explained by pointing out the simple or elementary causes or tendencies from what it results; as the motion of the earth and other planets round the sun is explained on the supposition of a rectilinear projectile, or tangential force, combined with the tendency to the centre. We know that two such tendencies would produce such an effect; and as we have proofs of the one, we allow the other. But the elementary tendencies themselves cannot be explained, they can only be ascertained to be real, and to be generally diffused; and when a case of them occurs, as when a stone falls to the ground, all we can say is, that it is a particular instance of a general tendency, not an isolated fact. Here we generalize, but we do not assign a cause. These tendencies, which cannot be determined to be the result of more general causes, are sometimes called ultimate facts, as well as laws, and they are properly inexplicable, *i. e.* they cannot be *unfolded* and shown to be compound results of more simple tendencies. Such are Cohesion, Gravity, and the three Laws of Motion.

We have shown that the division of Causes into Immediate and Remote, differs from that into Proximate and Ultimate. Accordingly, there is another way of explaining by causes; and instead of ascending in the scale of generalization from compound and palpable causes to simple and concealed, we may trace the order of the former, from the last effect up to the most remote cause, in other words, the sequence of causation. Thus, starting from the movement of the hands on the dial-plate of a watch, we may follow the series of motions through wheels and other mechanical contrivances up to the first power, the spring. So, the process of digestion in the animal frame may be traced from the mastication of the food in the mouth, till it is converted into chyme and chyle, and finally lost in the blood.

But, when with a wish to enlarge our knowledge, we enquire what is the cause of motion in all watches, or in all clocks, we find that, in the one case, the general cause is that tendency in certain bodies which we call elasticity, in the other gravity:

while, as to digestion and nutrition, the general causes of these results are, as yet, involved in much obscurity; though the series of sensible changes, the uniform sequence of phenomena, can be traced throughout.

These different modes of explanation agree in this, that they assign a cause of one sort or another. But the word explanation is sometimes used when no cause at all is pointed out. It is so used when we profess to account for some effect by means of a general law of which it is merely a particular instance; as when we think to explain the fall of a stone, by saying that it is owing to gravity. This is a case of gravity certainly; and if so, it cannot at the same time be the effect thereof. But this sense of the word *explanation* is very common in works of philosophy, though it cannot be considered a proper one, for it differs essentially from the other, and so leads to much misconception. No doubt, even in this way of explaining, a great truth may be enounced; for instance, that the fall of an apple from a tree is an effect not singular in nature, but a particular case of a tendency common to all matter. This was the grand generalization of Newton. To explain the tendency itself, he supposed the existence of a fluid called ether; but this conjecture has met with little favour,[1] and gravity is still an

[1] The hypothesis of the existence of ether has been revived of

ultimate and unaccountable fact. It is not however a barren fact; for though itself an effect inexplicable, it is also a mighty cause, which helps to account for the more complicated phenomena of the universe, for the movements of a common clock, as well as the revolutions of Jupiter and Uranus.

Though Newton failed in discovering the whole cause of the grand tendency, gravitation, yet he may be considered as having made some approximation towards it, when he determined the circumstances which regulate the force of the tendency; for he proved that the force varies directly as the quantity of matter, and inversely as the squares of the distances. Therefore the quantity of matter and the distance being given, the resulting force may be determined. So far the cause of gravity is known; and this knowledge may lead to the most important discoveries. This it was which led Adams and Le Verrier to the grand discovery of the new planet. It was from the perturbations of Uranus that those profound inquirers not only suspected the existence of a planet beyond, but even assigned its position, magnitude, and distance from the sun, before it was seen by mortal eye. For those perturbations implied a disturbing force, and this force implied as the cause a certain quantity of matter at a certain

late years in order to explain light, which upon this supposition consists in *Vibrations of Ether.*

distance, in other words, a planet of a determined mass, removed from Uranus by a determined space.

The law of the proportions in which bodies combine, or, as it is now usually called by chemists, the Atomic Theory, is another grand instance of a general effect, or tendency to an effect, of which the cause is unknown; though an attempt has been made to account for that effect also by means of an hypothesis. To have discovered that when one body enters into combination with another in different proportions, the greater proportions are always exact multiples of the smallest, was certainly a grand step in the science of chemistry; but this is only a general effect; to explain which, that is to assign a cause for it, Dalton hit upon atoms, as Newton imagined ether to account for gravitation.

Before concluding this article, we may remark that the phrase, *Law of Nature,* is often employed in a more extensive sense than the one here given, being used to signify any general fact, any general uniformity of succession, whether the cause be stated or not; or even, as it appears, any uniformity of co-existence. Thus the laws, as they are called, of Kepler, tell us nothing concerning causes; they merely state some general facts with respect to the motions of the planets; for instance, that they move in elliptical orbits, without pretending to explain them. These and others similar are sometimes called Empirical Laws.[k] In this sense the perpetual recurrence of day and night, of night and day, may be called a law of nature.

Lastly, were we to say that it is a law of nature that all warm blooded animals have internal lungs, we should be thought to use no unwarrantable language; though here we state mere uniformity of co-existence, without any reference to motion or change, much less to causation.

It is necessary, therefore, to bear in mind that *Law*, *Law of Phenomena*, and even *Law of Nature*, are frequently used to signify any uniformity, whether of succession or of co-existence, and whether a cause be apparent or not.

And we must remember that the word *explanation* is not always used in its proper sense of assigning a cause, but often where there is generalization only, where a fact is classed as a particular instance of one more general, or of a Law in its widest sense. Thus, when Kelper deduced from the observed positions of the planets, that they move in elliptical orbits, he might be said to *explain* those positions; though the explanation amounted simply to this, that the observed positions were particular points of the general figure ellipse, which embraced them all.

[k] By Dr. Whewell they are called *Laws of Phenomena*, and as such, are distinguished from the *Causes* of Phenomena.—See " Philosophy of the Inductive Sciences." Book xi. chap. 7.

# PRINCIPLE.

WHAT are we to understand by that word of so frequent occurrence, Principle?

One meaning of principle certainly is a *General or Ultimate Cause*, as when we talk of the principle of heat, of magnetism, of electricity, meaning thereby the unknown cause of certain well-known phenomena, such as expansion, a peculiar sensation, the attraction of iron, a violent shock to the frame, &c. So we art wont to talk of the principle of life, the thinking principle, &c.

In chemistry, the word principle is sometimes used in its proper signification of general or ultimate cause, as when we speak of Tannin or the tanning principle; morphia or the narcotic principle; quinine or the anti-febrile principle. In these cases we can actually produce the cause as a substance, and operate therewith.

But in chemistry, the word principle is more frequently used in another sense, as when we mention the proximate principles of animal and vegetable substances, such as gluten, gelatin, albumen, &c. Here the word Principle means *constituent part* or *ingredient*, that which serves to make up the more compound substances, muscle, cellular tissue, and the rest. Constituent parts or ingredients, when we can analyze them no further, are called ultimate principles or elements, as the metals, oxygen, hydrogen, and chlorine gases.

Though these two senses of the word Principle are not the same, yet it is evident that the same substance may unite the two characteristics, that it may be at once a cause and a constituent part. Thus morphia is a constituent part of opium, and likewise the cause of its narcotic effects. So with quinine, strychnia, &c., which are chemical ingredients of bark, and nux vomica, and also the sources of their medical virtues.

In pure metaphysics generally, and in moral and political sciences very frequently, the word Principle is used in its proper, primary, or original sense. Thus, when Montesquieu maintains that virtue is the principle of democracies, moderation of aristocracies, honour of monarchies, he means that such are the *causes* which preserve each of these sorts of government, or, which are essential to their prosperity and continuance. So when we talk of liberty, activity, variety, and contrast, as principles of human happiness, we mean that they are general causes of the same. In a like sense we say that division of labour is a principle favourable to the increase of wealth. The discovery of such principles is the highest object of philosophy.

But in religion, morals, and politics, principles are sometimes distinguished into speculative and practical; the former relating to the existence of things as they are, the other to things as they may be, or ought to be. When we say that moral sentiment springs from sympathy and reason, we state a speculative principle, but when we affirm that moral sentiment ought to be regulated by views of far-sighted and comprehensive utility, we lay down a practical principle, as it is often called, or rule of action.

In this case, the rule is a moral one, that is, it tends to regulate the emotions so as to produce happiness: but there may also be rules for directing the understanding, or logical rules. What is essential to a rule is, that it point out something whereby practice may be improved; meaning by practice, not merely outward actions, but also the play of emotions, and likewise the exercise of the intellect.

A rule then acts, or is intended to act, either on the understanding or the emotions, or rather on the understanding always in the first instance, and then, if it be a moral rule, on the emotions.

In this sense, Principle is not synonymous with General Cause, but with general reason. And as all rules are stated in the form of general propositions, a practical principle or rule may be defined to be—

*A general proposition, intended to direct the understanding, or the emotions, or both.*

In this sense, we talk of a man of liberal principles, or of religious principles, meaning that the rules which direct his understanding, his emotions, and probably his actions, are of the kind designated by these epithets.

Sometimes any general proposition, supposed to be pregnant with consequences, is called a Principle. Thus Locke begins his essay with an account of what he calls speculative principles, such as " it is impossible for the same thing to be and not to be ;" but the proper name is *Axiom*. In a like sense, the major premiss of a syllogism, according to Archbishop Whately, is sometimes called the principle.[1]

This meaning of the word as well as the preceding, seem to have arisen from a supposed analogy between the relation of a general cause to its particular effects, and that of a general proposition to the particular conclusions that may be drawn from it. But these are very different relations; and the use of the same word to express both is apt to lead to great confusion.

From the above detail, it appears that the word Principle may mean either an ultimate cause, or a

---

[1] Elements of Logic, Book i. Sec. 2. But the able Reviewer of Whately's Logic, Edinburgh Review, No. cxv., says, that the major premiss is often called the Proposition, never the Principle.

constituent part, whether proximate or ultimate, of any compound, that which helps to make it up; or a rule to direct us; or even a general proposition of any kind, from which consequences logically flow. In this latter sense, we talk of the principles of a science, as the principles of morals, of political economy, &c.; meaning the most important, the fundamental propositions, from which the rest may be deduced. Though it is vain to suppose that we can accurately limit the sense of words in daily use, yet in philosophy we may be more precise, and ought to be so, for without precision of language there is no science. I would therefore exclude principle from a philosophical vocabulary, in the sense either of rule, or axiom, or general proposition of any kind, from which particular consequences flow.

Omitting, for the present at least, these significations as improper, we shall then find that the term Principle, besides the notion of generality, always has a reference to origin, and hence implies priority; for though we certainly cannot prove that the elements of any compound existed before the compound, yet we suppose so, and having first the elements, we can in many cases unite them so as afterwards to obtain a new product; as when from copper and zinc we obtain a new substance, brass. Where then Principle does not mean cause, in the proper sense of the word, or the indispensable antecedent of some change, it at least means that which is essential to the being of any thing, that which is supposed to have preceded the existence of something else, and without which the latter could never have been. It is on account of this supposed priority, that the term Principle is applied to the elements of bodies, as well as to the causes of manifest changes in matter or in mind. This notion of priority then belongs essentially to Principle. The two notions then essential to Principle, are generality and priority; and accordingly it may be defined to be *that from which many particular things originate, or at least are supposed to originate; that without the prior existence of which many particular things could not be.*

In this sense, Principle comprehends two species.

Active Principle or Cause, and Constituent Principle.

Now were we to allow the word Principle in the sense of general proposition leading to particular conclusions, what analogy could we find between this and the other signification just given? Generality, no doubt, belongs to both, and even priority, *in a certain sense*, inasmuch as a general proposition is a premiss from which conclusions follow. But it is evident that this is a very different sort of priority from the real priority of a cause to its effect; it is in technical language, a Subjective, not an Objective priority; or, in plain words, it is a priority in reference to our view of it, while the other is a real priority in the phenomena themselves. We must first see the general proposition, before we can draw the inference, and in that sense it is prior, and in no other.

This distinction must be kept in mind, in case we persist in using the word principle to signify a general premiss. If that sense be retained, though generality and even priority in a certain sense may still be the characteristics of a principle; yet we must draw a line between the genera, which will be two in number; namely,

I. A general and ultimate cause, from which many effects follow; or else, an elementary body from which compounds result.

II. A general proposition from which, as premiss, particular conclusions follow.

The first is either a purely metaphysical or a physical Principle, as the case may be; the latter is a logical Principle.

Lastly. A Principle, whether metaphysical or physical, comprehends, as we have seen, two species:

1. Active Principle or Cause.
2. Constituent Principle: while a logical Principle is either speculative or practical, otherwise called rule, according to the division of Locke.

Those Principles or general propositions which expressly direct our thoughts, emotions, and actions, are called practical; while those that do not are speculative: in other words, speculative principles relate to the existence of things as they are, practical, to things as they may be or ought to be; as before illustrated by the case of speculative and practical principles of morals.

## A REASON.

What is called a Reason is a cause of a peculiar sort, a cause suited to act on the understanding, so as to produce conviction, or a lower degree of belief. The question, why do I approve of such an action? may mean either what is the cause that actually rouses my sentiment of approbation, or else, what is the reason (or cause) which on reflection fixes my conviction of the worthiness of the actor, and hence tends to rouse emotion in his favour? It certainly may happen that these two causes coincide, but they also may differ.

Why did Cæsar overthrow the constitution of his country? Through ambition or desire of power. Why was Tiberius a tyrant? or why do you call him a tyrant? Because he perpetrated arbitrary and cruel acts. The former is evidently a cause, usually so called; the other a reason, or a cause of my opinion. The one sort of causes may be called physical, or metaphysical, as the case may be; the other logical, being addressed solely to the understanding. Another classification would be to divide causes into the physical, and the mental or metaphysical; and then to subdivide the latter into pure metaphysical and logical causes, otherwise called Reasons. But it is more agreeable to the real distinctions of things, to divide causes into causes proper, and reasons, or logical causes; the former being subdivided into the physical and the mental or metaphysical.

Sometimes, however, a reason means the final cause, or purpose. Why, or what is the reason that the eye has a lens, means this. But final causes, as we have seen, are, in reality, effects; and they are called causes only because the foresight of such effects is supposed to have created a motive in the mind of the Deity to provide means adapted to the end in view. Therefore final causes, if they be entitled to be called causes at all, are of the nature of reasons; they are the supposed reasons of the Deity for such and such creations.

Having determined that a Reason generally means that which acts on the understanding, and produces belief, it is easy to see that this, when expressed in words, must be a proposition; for propositions alone are addressed to the intellectual faculties. And as those are supposed to influence the understanding, therefore they partake of the nature of causes. But they must be carefully distinguished from causes physical, as well as from causes purely metaphysical. Now a proposition from which we draw an inference, is called, in logical language, a premiss; and hence we see that a reason expressed in words, and a premiss, are the same.

Were we to adopt that distinction before pointed out, between the *objective* and the *subjective*, then causes, properly so called, would be objective, and reasons subjective; for the former relate to the being of things *in themselves*, the latter to *our way of knowing* them. In short, a cause physical, or one purely metaphysical, is the indispensable antecedent of any event; a cause logical, or reason, is the indispensable antecedent of our belief of that event.

Though the above be, as we conceive, the proper use of the word Reason, yet we cannot assert that it is the only one; for reason is often put for cause physical or purely metaphysical. Thus one might ask, without any flagrant departure from the common use of words, what is the reason that Sirius twinkles and Jupiter not? meaning, what is the physical cause? But it is vain to attempt to tie down the common use of words, all we can hope to do is to fix their philosophical sense, and to shew that a certain analogy runs through all the senses, though it may be far-fetched. Thus, in the present instance, we have shewn that a reason, after all, is a cause of a peculiar sort.

## SCIENCE AND PHILOSOPHY.

Science differs from other knowledge, in this, that it is the knowledge of *general facts,* i. e. facts common to many individual existences. Civil history, and geography, so far as mere topography, are not sciences, because the knowledge they give is particular; the history of one kingdom not being the history of another; the geography of this country not being the geography of that. The history of Rome is not the same as that of Greece; nor the geography of England as that of Italy. This is the reason why civil history and geography are so lengthy. A man may read history all his life, and still have very much to learn. No doubt, sciences, such as physical geography in its general bearings, and politics, may be founded on these, but in themselves they are not sciences.

Natural history, however, *is* science, because the facts of which it treats are general, or common to innumerable particular existences. When we describe and class a horse, or an elephant, we describe and class all horses, or all elephants.[m]

[m] Hence we see the great imperfection of Bacon's classification in this particular; for he considers natural history as no science at all, as requiring only an effort of memory, and he arranges it along with civil history as a species of the same genus. The

Natural history, in all its branches is principally a science of description and classification; and therefore it does not come up to the dignity of philosophy. For all science is not entitled to the name of philosophy, though all philosophy be science.

I. What then, are the peculiar objects of philosophical enquiry?

In order to answer this important and difficult question, let us consider that everything in nature may be regarded in two points of view; as existing with or without reference to what went before or what will come after; that is, with or without reference to time. In the one case, the objects of inquiry are considered as co-existing, in the other as successive; there we wish to know them as they are at the present moment, without change; here, as preceded or followed by other phenomena.

Agreeably to this well marked distinction, and according to what was said above, that science treats of *general* truths, we find that the object of all science is two-fold, viz:—

To discover uniformities of co-existence and uniformities of succession in nature.

common use of language seems to have led him into this mistake. There may be some analogy between civil and natural history, according to which they have, in ordinary language, been classed together, but this analogy is not sufficient for an exact classification.

Commencing with uniformities of co-existence, or in other words, the constitution of nature, we shall find that these uniformities are of two sorts, the palpable or apparent, and the latent or hidden. The former we may discover by our senses, with or without artificial assistance, including proper instruments, while the latter can be ascertained only by reflection, or by a peculiar agency called chemical, which operates upon the insensible particles of matter. Thus the different tissues and the different organs of a horse or a dog can be separated by anatomical skill, and seen by anybody, as may the parts of a rose or a tulip; but the *intimate* composition of these parts and organs can be detected only by a power which shall resolve them into their elements. Now, though it is the object of science in general to trace both these sorts of co-existence, yet we conceive that to philosophy alone, properly so called, it appertains to determine the *intimate* composition of things. But natural history treats of *palpable* co-existence alone, and therefore, so far at least as co-existence is concerned, it is a branch of science, but not of philosophy. To philosophy, then, belongs the knowledge of the intimate composition of things.

But things are of two grand sorts, mental and bodily, or spiritual and material. Therefore one grand object of philosophy is the discovery, by analysis, of the intimate composition of things existing, whether bodies or mental phenomena.[n]

The sciences employed upon this object are pure mental science, or metaphysics, and chemistry; the one having reference to mind, the other to bodies or material substances. Thus, we find out by chemistry that the air we breathe is compounded of three elements, oxygen gas, nitrogen or azote, and a very small quantity of carbonic acid gas: while by metaphysical analysis we discover that love, and some other passions, are made up of various elementary feelings.

II. The next grand object of science is to determine uniformities of succession, or in other words, the course of nature. Now, in treating of cause and effect, we remarked that there are some uniformities of succession in which the events are connected together as cause and effect, and others in which they are not; and we instanced the succession of day and night, night and day, as one quite uniform, but not a case of causation. Many other cases are there where the successive changes may depend in some degree one upon another, as cause and effect, though we know not in what degree; but the probability is, that like the suc-

---

[n] So far as bodies are concerned, this is called by Bacon the *Latens Schematismus*.

cession of day and night, they depend chiefly upon one or two general causes, modified by circumstances, that is, by auxiliary or secondary causes, such as the palpable changes immediately preceding. Thus, the growth of man from infancy to childhood, from childhood to youth, from youth to manhood, is a long series of changes, uniform in all; of changes every one of which may be indispensable to the next following, but still contributing to it only in a small degree; the principal cause of growth being hid far from our view. In tracing the changes that go on during digestion, we follow the food from the mouth to the stomach, where it meets with the gastric juice, and is changed into *Chyme;* from the stomach to the smaller bowels, where it meets with the bile and the pancreatic juice, and becomes *Chyle;* from the bowels to the lacteal vessels, by which it communicates with the blood, when digestion is completed. The whole of these changes constitutes the *process* of digestion. So, the discovery of Harvey consisted in tracing the blood from the *left* side of the heart, into the great vessel, the aorta; from the aorta by perpetual subdivision into innumerable small arteries; from these back again by veins, at first numberless and minute, but at last all uniting into one, and pouring their contents into the *right* side of the heart. From this right side, Harvey again traced the blood, issuing in one great trunk, to be subdivided in the lungs into ten thousand branches, which afterwards re-unite and discharge the fluid by one vessel into the *left* side of the heart. Thus is the circulation completed. In these and similar instances, it will be observed that there is no attempt to trace general causes; there is only a *history* of successive phenomena.

Let us now take an instance from chemistry. When we are introduced for the first time into a chemist's laboratory, we are surprised at the various changes that ensue on his mixing different substances together, but we feel to have no knowledge until he has explained to us the *latent process*. He shows us a fluid now clear as water, into which he pours another fluid equally clear; when suddenly an inward commotion is perceived; bubbles of gas rise to the surface, and at last there is found at the bottom of the glass a solid substance. Then he informs us that the original liquid contained, in solution, a salt, compounded of carbonic acid and an earth or oxide; that the other liquid was a stronger acid, which combined with the earth or oxide, and forming an insoluble compound, fell to the bottom; while the carbonic acid, being set free, ascended through the liquid and mixed with the atmosphere.

Now we feel to know something, for the *latent process*, or sequence of phenomena, has been laid open to us. Still, in all this there is no attempt to trace general causes. No doubt, in knowing this sequence we do know something of causation, inasmuch as we know some change indispensable to the next following; but this change is but the proximate, not the ultimate or general cause.

Now, the knowledge of the uniform sequences of phenomena is an important part of science, whether these be sequences of causation or not. Sometimes, as in the case of the succession of day and night, there is no relation of power between the two successive events; at other times there may be some relation, the preceding change being a secondary or a proximate cause of the following change; but be that as it may, the knowledge of uniform sequence is interesting and important, though it be not the highest object of science. The sciences which treat of these sequences are natural history and concrete chemistry, so far as they treat of sequence at all; for, as we have seen, another object of these sciences is to trace the constitution of bodies, apparent and latent. Natural history, then, treats of the apparent or sensible constitution or structure of bodies, as well as of the sensible processes or changes which they undergo, without tracing these to general causes; while concrete chemistry investigates the hidden or insensible constitution of bodies, and likewise the latent processes which they go through when different substances are brought into contact. Thus, natural history consists of two parts, one of which describes the sensible constitution or structure of bodies, and arranges them accordingly into classes, orders, genera, and species; while the other traces the sensible changes which they undergo, and, at most, the proximate causes of those changes. On natural history, as its foundation, arises the philosophy of natural history, which attempts to trace general causes.

The philosophy of zoology is commonly called physiology; of botany, physiological botany; of mineralogy, and physical geography, of fossil zoology and fossil botany, geology is the philosophy; of descriptive astronomy, physical astronomy.

The differences in the outward form and colour of animals are of much less importance than differences in their inward structure; and they are also more variable in the same species. But the former are visible to all, and are therefore remarked; while the latter can be known only by dissection and patient examination. Often, with a striking difference in outward appearances, we can connect no sensible differences in the inward structure. How different in appearance is a pug dog from a Newfoundland, a Shetland pony from a race horse; much more a horse from an ass, a sheep from a goat; but we can trace no difference in anatomy. There is then a loose distinction in descriptive zoology between the strict and the popular; the former treating of the sensible though inward structure of animals, and of the sensible though inward changes which they undergo; while the latter dwells chiefly upon their outward form and colour, their movements, their habits of life, their relations with other animals, &c. Thus, the *Regne Animal* of Cuvier contains only a short characteristic description of each animal, founded on its anatomical structure, and sufficient to distinguish it from all other species: while the great work of Buffon is an amusing literary production, embracing all that he knew about animals, their modes of life, instincts, and dispositions. Such, also, is Goldsmith's Animated Nature. Works of this kind, though not very exact, may still be called works of science, inasmuch as they treat of general facts—facts common to all species, or at least to the greater number; though they have no pretension to the name of philosophy; for they investigate neither the concealed elements, nor the hidden causes of things.

Here it may not be out of place to consider from what analogy, civil and natural history have been classed together as species of the same genus, not only in common language, but even in the arrangement of Bacon.

Simple civil history, or annals, consist of a narrative or relation of *particular* facts, either successive in the same place, or contemporaneous in different places, with as little reference to causes as may be; for it is scarcely possible to relate events without some suggestion concerning their causes—their palpable or proximate causes at least. The tracing of the hidden or ultimate causes of events belongs to the philosophy of history.

Natural history, on the other hand, relates *general* facts, facts common to whole classes, orders, genera, or species at the lowest; facts either simultaneous, as the parts of an animal or a plant shown by dissection, or else successive, as the circulation of the blood and the process of digestion. The knowledge of simultaneous facts is one of position only, not of causation at all; and even the knowledge of an uniform sequence may give us little insight into causes, at least into general causes. These last are the object of the philosophy of natural history, of physiology, geology, and physical astronomy. Such is the analogy between civil and natural history, and such the difference. Both, when properly called *history*, relate facts, simultaneous or successive, as simply as possible, without tracing hidden causes; but the facts in the one case are *particular*, in the other *general*. Therefore, the one is *science*, the other not. Let us take two instances to illustrate the above distinctions, the one from civil, the other from natural history. No historian, no mere annalist, can relate the events which preceded the great American war without mentioning the stamp act and the duty on tea, as causes of the outbreak. These are causes which strike every one, even the least clear-sighted; they are then *palpable* or *proximate*. But the philosophic historian will stop his narrative for a moment to inquire into the more hidden causes of the war, the causes which predisposed the American mind to so decided a step; and this he will probably determine to be the yearning of a people, now no longer in infancy, for independence and political importance. This, then, was the ultimate cause, and it is also a general one, not confined to this particular case, but operating among different nations at different times.

Again, in tracing the process of digestion, it is easy to see that the teeth, the saliva, the gastric juice, the mascular motion of the stomach, the bile, and the pancreatic juice, all produce certain changes in the food, changes evident to the senses, and universally attributed to the above as causes, to a certain extent at least; for without them the same changes would not ensue; but we cannot doubt that there are more hidden causes at work, upon which the vitality of all these agents, and the peculiar effects of each depend. The former causes are palpable or proximate, and a subject merely for history; the latter, hidden or ultimate, and they belong to the philosophy of the science, that is, to physiology.

Here it must be observed, however, that as classes nearly related are apt to run one into another, so, simple or descriptive natural history of animals for instance, and physiology, cannot always be clearly distinguished. So far as natural history treats of structure only, of what is simultaneous and not successive, it is quite distinct from the philosophy of natural history, which investigates general causes. But when natural history relates uniform sequences of phenomena, it cannot always avoid mentioning causes of some sort; and here, therefore, it will sometimes be confounded with philosophy. Uniform sequences then are the ground where descriptive natural history and philosophy meet. The more apparent sequences would by all be attributed to the former, such as the outward changes which animals undergo from their birth to maturity, from maturity to old age; their different movements, their modes of life, and their relations to each other; but the inward and more concealed changes, such as take place in digestion, may be said to belong to physiology. Indeed, they generally are so considered, though when related as known facts without any theory, without reference to general causes, they belong more properly to history.

Physiology, then, as generally understood, comprehends more than what can well be called philosophy. It is the science of function, as opposed to structure, and treats of the actions or uses of all the organs of the body, from the most apparent to the most concealed, from the contraction of the muscles, to the very obscure agency of the brain, nerves, and ganglia. It treats of causes of all kinds operating within the frame, whether they be palpable and proximate, such as the saliva which softens the food, the gastric juice which dissolves it, the bile which changes it still more, the synovia which moistens the joints, &c. &c.; or whether they be hidden and ultimate, such as the general causes of the heat of the body, of nutrition, motion, and sensation. These last form certainly one of the most difficult subjects for human inquiry.

The highest, that is, the most important and the most difficult object of science, is the discovery of *hidden*, *ultimate*, or *general* causes, for all these words apply to the same thing; and to the search after such causes, the name of Philosophy has always been given. These causes never present themselves open and naked before us; they are always surrounded, as it were, by a thick veil, which hides them from our eyes. To pierce this veil, to tear asunder this covering, is then our grand object, and our grand difficulty.

The proper name for these causes, as we have seen, is *principle*, or *active principle*, to distinguish them from the hidden elements of things, considered merely as component parts, to which we have given the name of *constituent principle*. The knowledge of principles, then, in both these senses, is the object of Philosophy as distinguished from other Science. We have already illustrated the meaning of principle, by reference to quinine, morphia, and strychnia, which are, at one and the same time, component parts of bark, opium, and nux vomica, and the real or hidden causes of their medicinal effects. We may now also mention bitter almonds and bay leaves, the poisonous influence of which depends upon a minute quantity of prussic acid present in those substances. No science affords us illustrations better adapted for our present purpose than that of chemistry. Chemical science is generally divided into two parts; the first treating of all the particular substances in Nature, their intimate composition, and the hidden changes which they undergo when brought into contact with each other, in other words, the *latentes schematismi*, and the *latentes processus;* the second, investigating the effects of certain general principles or causes, widely diffused throughout nature, such as caloric and electricity. These principles are known from their effects, but we cannot arrest and examine them by themselves; and it is even disputed whether caloric be a peculiar matter, or merely a modification of ordinary matter.

Some of the greatest discoveries consist not in the detection of any new principle, but in generalising and diminishing the number of principles or causes already known, or rather inferred; for often from their effects alone we know them. When Franklin drew down lightning from the clouds, he did not discover the existence of any new principle; he proved that the phenomena of lightning and those of electricity excited by our machines, depend upon one and the same cause; yet this is looked upon as one of the greatest discoveries of modern times. So, should philosophers succeed in establishing the identity of the principle of electricity and that of magnetism, this also would be a great discovery.

From these examples, drawn from the material world, we may judge what is meant by general causes or principles in the world of mind. Since the beginning of authentic history, we everywhere hear of the poverty of the mass of the people. The prophecy, "the poor shall never cease out of the land," has amply been fulfilled. Poverty has existed, more or less, not only in cold climates, but in the warmest and most genial; not only in barren countries, but in the most fertile; not only under despotic sway, but under free and constitutional governments; not only among barbarous nations, ignorant of the arts of life, but among the most polished and civilized, well acquainted with implements and machinery to facilitate the production of wealth; finally, not only among indolent people, but even among the most industrious. Poverty is known among the hard-working population of Manchester, as well as among the wild inhabitants of Connemara. These facts had been present to man for a long series of ages; and though some may have guessed the real cause of the mischief, it was reserved for MALTHUS to *prove*, that the principle of population, that is, the *tendency* of population to increase faster than subsistence, is the grand general cause of the poverty and misery of the people. Surely such a man ought to be considered as great a benefactor to mankind as the most sublime mathematician and astronomer that ever lived.

Though this principle is not an ultimate one, for it can be traced to more general principles; yet it is not the less valuable on that account, and it forms a good illustration of the remark of Bacon, that *principia media* are often more fruitful than *principia generalissima*.

The ultimate object of philosophy is the discovery of the *general laws of nature;* that is, as we formerly explained, of general effects, or tendencies to effects, which, as such, cannot be traced to any cause, being themselves the most general causes, that we know, of the other and more complicated phenomena of the universe. Such are gravitation, cohesion, and the three laws of motion. All these are inexplicable, at least for the present, that is, we know not their causes, but they are themselves causes acting universally. Thus, at length, after all our labour, we arrive at facts which we cannot explain, except upon a supposition of a self-existent, first cause. It is like the world supported on a tortoise, the tortoise on an elephant, the elephant on a whale;

but what supports the whale? There we are stopped short. We are as far from a satisfactory explanation as ever.

Taking this into consideration, what shall we think of the wisdom of those philosophers, those famous physical astronomers, who think, when they have found out a general law, that there is no longer any occasion for a law giver? Do they not perceive that their boasted law is itself an effect requiring explanation as much as any other; and that the only rational questions are, first, whether any cause thereof be traceable by us; and secondly, whether ultimately we must rest on a material or a spiritual first cause? in other words, whether matter arranged itself into the most beautiful and beneficial order, or whether this was the work of mind? Do not these philosophers see that the law which they have discovered, far from weakening the proofs of an intelligent first cause, decidedly strengthens them? for a law supposes order, and order argues design, and design a designer; so that unless the law made itself we must have recourse to Deity.

But so natural, so unavoidable, is the idea of a Great Intelligent First Cause, that those who deny the same in words have been obliged to admit His existence, though in a covert manner. For this purpose, the term *Nature* has been found convenient; and instead of saying that such and such phenomena are the work of God, they pronounce them the work of Nature, thus substituting a metaphorical person for a real; for the word *Nature* properly means the very effects to be explained; which are thus put for the one great and unseen Cause of all.

In concluding this article, I may observe that whether the sense I have given to *Philosophy*, as distinguished from other Science, be generally approved or not, yet the statement as to the objects of all Science will not be thereby affected. That statement may be correct, whatever more limited sense we attach to the term Philosophy.

# HYPOTHESIS AND THEORY.

As no words occur more frequently in philosophy than these, it is necessary to fix their meaning, if possible, with accuracy.

Hypothesis and Theory agree in this, that they both pretend to explain phenomena, in other words, they assign a cause or the causes thereof. We cannot, therefore, be surprised that those words should occur so often in philosophy, which has for its special object to discover the causes of things. And as causes, as we have seen, are of different sorts, so there may be as many hypotheses, or as many theories corresponding, relative to the immediate, or the remote, the proximate, or the ultimate cause.

Secondly, Hypothesis and Theory agree also in this, that both imply more or less of uncertainty as to the accuracy of the explanation; for when the investigation is thought complete, and all doubt is at an end, Theory is changed into Fact. Theory is not distinguished from Fact by the circumstance that the one enounces a cause, the other not; for though a fact may imply no cause, yet it frequently does imply one. Thus, when I say that I can move my arm when I will,

I state what every one would call a fact, though this fact implies that my will is the cause of the motion. So when I affirm that heat and moisture are causes of vegetation, I state what all will allow to be facts, just as much as when I inform any one that the heart of man contains four cavities, and that the chest is separated from the abdomen by a muscle called the diaphram or midriff, facts relative to structure only, not to causation. Hypothesis and Theory differ then from Fact in this, that they imply some uncertainty with respect to the causes assigned, while Fact supposes none.

Thus far Hypothesis and Theory agree; but, wherein do they differ?

There is no very definite distinction between Hypothesis and Theory. The distinction, such as it is, turns entirely upon the degree of evidence possessed by each respectively; for an Hypothesis is only a doubtful Theory; and, on further investigation, and by means of new evidence, the former may be raised to the dignity of the latter. Thus, as we pass from Theory to Fact involving causation, so do we pass from Hypothesis to Theory, according as the cause in question is doubtful, probable, or certain; Hypothesis being at one end of the series, and Fact at the other.

From the above it follows, that in many cases,

it may be difficult to say whether the term Hypothesis or the term Theory be most applicable. But in other cases there can be no doubt. Where the existence of the supposed cause, in the case in question, rests only upon some faint analogy, and still more where such a cause is not known with certainty to exist in *any* case, there we have only an Hypothesis. Thus the *Vortices* of Descartes were hypothetical, because though some sort of *Vortices*, as whirl-pools, were known to exist, yet the analogy between these motions and those of the earth and planets was very far-fetched. So the nervous vibrations of Hartley, to which he attributed the phenomena of sensation, were purely hypothetical; for what analogy is there between a nerve and a musical chord? In like manner, some physiologists have attributed all the phenomena of life to mechanical causes known to exist, others to chemical alone; as if the human frame were either a mere machine, or a mere laboratory. Nay, such has been the wildness of Hypothesis, that the world itself has sometimes been supposed to be an animal, sometimes even a God.

In other instances, a cause not known with certainty, or even with probability, to exist in *any* case, is supposed, in order to account for some phenomena. Thus, Newton imagined that the phenomena of gravitation might be accounted for by the impulse of an unknown substance, which he called Ether; and some philosophers in the present day attribute the phenomena of light to the vibrations of the same mysterious fluid. But as the existence of Ether in any case has never been shown by the proper proofs, by the only proofs by which we can in the first instance ascertain the existence of any body, namely, by the senses; as no one has ever seen, touched, smelt, heard, or tasted Ether, we have a right to say that it exists only hypothetically. The proper evidence of the existence of matter, in the first instance, is sense, or more correctly, perception; that of the existence of spirit is consciousness. We believe in the existence of our own spirit, and of other spirits around us, and above us, which we have not seen; for spirits cannot be seen or touched, and there are other proofs of their existence; but we are not justified in believing implicitly in any species of matter which no one has ever descried by the senses.

For the same reason, the existence of caloric and electricity, as distinct sorts of matter, is hypothetical. They are called *Imponderable;* but what kind of matter can that be which has no weight? For a long time, sensation and muscular motion were attributed to *animal spirits,* a fluid remarkably rare and volatile, which was supposed to be always flying about between the brain and the organs of sensation and motion; but as no one has been able to detect this fluid, its existence, which was always hypothetical, is now disbelieved altogether. In the present day, atoms find more favour, and on them is founded a famous Theory; but as no one has seen or touched such particles, we may be allowed to doubt their existence, and call it hypothetical.

In these and similar instances, we see a marked distinction between Hypothesis, Theory, and Fact; for no one could compare the Theory of gravitation with the Hypothesis of ether; or the Fact of muscular motion simply by means of nerves, with the supposition of animal spirits. That muscular motion is performed, some how or other, by means of the nerves, is an established Fact involving causation; that all bodies tend to each other, is a Theory; that the cause of this tendency is the impulse of a subtle fluid, Ether, is an Hypothesis. But the only difference between these three consists in the degree of evidence on which our belief is founded.

Though Hypotheses be in their nature doubtful, yet are they far from useless. The use of Hypothesis is not to terminate, but to direct inquiry; for our inquiry must have some object, something to prove, or disprove, and therefore a supposition or provisional solution may be necessary. We assume something to be true, and then observe, make experiments, and argue, to determine whether it be true. If our observation and experiments tally with the assumption, or if no absurd inferences follow from it, our Hypothesis may be raised into a Theory.

Though Hypotheses, properly so called, have no place in pure mathematics, which treat only of things co-existent, and not at all of causation, yet provisional assumptions are made, and the accuracy of them tested afterwards. Thus in the sixth proposition of Euclid, it is assumed, in the first instance, that the two sides which subtend two equal angles of a triangle, are not equal; and then, arguing on this supposition, we arrive at the absurd conclusion, that the less triangle is equal to the greater; whence we infer for certain that our assumption was false; and as there can here be but two suppositions, the other must be true. In mathematics, this mode of proof is quite satisfactory, because only two suppositions can be made, but in questions which admit of many solutions, where the boundaries of truth and falsehood are not strictly defined, there the disproof of one alternative proves not the other. Thus, were we to say that Cromwell was either an impostor or an enthusiast, and having proved him not to have been wholly an impostor, were we to conclude that he must have been wholly an enthusiast, our conclusion would not be certain, for he might have been partly the one, partly the other. We ought, therefore, in subjects which admit only of probability, always to distrust those arguments which are stated with mathematical precision, as in this form, either such a thing is, or is not; for generally there is a third alternative, which thus is kept out of sight.

Some may be unwilling to allow, that the only difference between Hypothesis, Theory, and Fact involving causation, consists in the degree of evidence on which they rest respectively. But if there be any other difference, I should like to know what it is. Theory, it may be said, is used to explain facts, to account for them; but what is meant by these phrases? To explain a phenomenon or fact, or to account for it, properly signifies, as we have seen, to point out the cause thereof; and the cause, when proved, must be another fact, or, until fully proved, a theory. Certainly, our speculative knowledge is thus enlarged, and possibly the cause may be one which we can apply to practice; but we are not to suppose that the fact explained is one whit less mysterious than before. It may be less anomalous, more akin to facts formerly known, but it is not the less incomprehensible.

Suppose it proved that gravitation is owing to impulses of ether, what do we learn by the discovery? We learn that gravitation is the effect of impact, that, therefore, it is a fact similar to others with which we are well acquainted, instead of being different from them. Thus, we simplify our knowledge, we reduce two modes of motion to one; but impulse, though more familiar, is quite as incomprehensible as attraction. It seems to us, no doubt, less mysterious, because it is more familiar; but this is a mere delusion, and the effect of custom. Why does one billiard ball, when put in motion, drive another before it? Could we have predicted such a result had we never seen it? Can we give any reason why it should be so? Or, if we could give a reason, what would it amount to? It would amount to this, either that some change intervenes between the impact of the one ball and the motion of the other, a change before unknown, a new fact or link in the chain of causation; or, that the real or ultimate cause of the motion is not impact, but something involved in the act of impact, something hidden from our sight, as morphia is hidden in the substance of opium. But whatever the explanation, the *why*, of impulse may be, it can be only the statement of some other fact as a cause; and not at all a reason, such as the reasoning of mathematics consists of, whereby we see, by the mind's eye, without actual experiment, that the angles at the base of an Isosceles triangle are and must be equal. All facts then involving causation are incomprehensible in this sense, that we can never see any *Reason*, properly so called, why any cause should produce any effect, or why it might not have produced one altogether different.

## METAPHYSICS, LOGIC, GRAMMAR,

### THEIR RESPECTIVE PROVINCES.

It is not a little remarkable, that, although so much has been said and written on the subject of Logic, from the days of Aristotle downwards, yet few branches of knowledge are so ill defined. By some, Logic is understood to embrace a very extensive territory, while by others, it has been restricted to very narrow limits. Thus, according to Watts, "Logic is the art of using REASON well in our enquiries after truth, and the communication of it to others." And in a note to this, we are told, "The word *Reason*, in this place, is not confined to the mere faculty of reasoning, or inferring one thing from another, but includes all the intellectual powers of man."

Against this definition, as too extensive and too vague, Archbishop Whately rebels; and says that "Logic, in the most extensive sense which the name can with propriety be made to bear, may be considered as the science, and also as the art of reasoning." According to this definition, which the author considers sufficiently extensive, several important subjects usually considered as belonging to Logic, are excluded from it, for instance, all appertaining to conceptions and names, to judgments and propositions, to definition and classification; though it appears from the work itself, of which the above is the opening sentence, that the author considered these subjects as comprised within the province of Logic. The definition, however, does not say so; and accordingly, this may be taken as a specimen, not of an enlarged, but on the contrary, of a very narrow definition, as that of Watts is of a very extensive one. Between these two extremes, a proper definition of Logic will probably be found. Moreover, Archbishop Whately seems to contradict what he had before laid down, when he says, that Logic is *entirely conversant about language*,° thereby lowering Logic to the level of Grammar, and breaking down the distinction between them; whereas, in the introduction, he had said that the "most appropriate office of Logic is that of instituting an analysis of the process of the mind in reasoning."

The third book of Whately's Logic treats of Fallacies; and a considerable part of it is taken up with what the author calls non-logical Fallacies. Why then, it may be asked, are they treated of in a work professedly on Logic? The

° See Whately's Logic, Book II. Sec. 2, note.

truth is, that the author is obliged to include more under Logic than he is willing to allow.

But if Whately's definition of Logic be narrow, that given by Barthélemy Saint Hilaire, the translator of Aristotle's Organon, is still more so. According to Saint Hilaire, Logic is a science, not an art, and the object of that science is demonstration. To justify this definition, the words of Aristotle at the commencement of the Prior Analytics are quoted. "First we shall mention the subject and the end of this study; the subject is demonstration; the end is science demonstrated."

Having first shown that Logic is a science, Saint Hilaire then inquires, what is the object of that science? To this question, Aristotle replies, "it is demonstration." "Nothing," says Saint Hilaire, "more simple nor more true than this answer."

If this be so, the limits of Logic are indeed narrow. For demonstration is to be found only in Mathematics, the science of quantity; therefore Logic treats only of Mathematical reasoning. But this is not true of any system of Logic with which we are acquainted. No writer on Logic confines himself to Mathematical reasoning; consequently demonstration is not the sole object of Logic, as universally understood. Reasoning, in general, not demonstrative reasoning only, is always included under Logic. But we must not suppose that the above is really given by Aristotle as a complete definition of Logic. It is the opening sentence of the Book, entitled Prior Analytics, and professes to state nothing more than the subject and end of that and the following Book, the Posterior Analytics, which treat indeed of Logic, but not of all Logic. We cannot, therefore, blame Aristotle for having given too narrow a definition of the whole science. Nay, further on, (Prior Analytics, Chap. IV.) Aristotle says expressly that the work on which he is engaged will comprehend more than demonstration; that it will contain the whole doctrine of the syllogism, which, says he, "is more general than demonstration, which is only a sort of syllogism, whereas every syllogism is not a demonstration." Hereupon he enters upon the syllogism, purporting to treat of demonstration afterwards, as he actually has done in the Posterior Analytics.

Of late, other definitions have been given of Logic, and by high authority. The very highest of all, on this subject, has defined Logic to be "The science of the formal laws of thought." With all due deference to that authority, I cannot but remark, that this definition, were it even correct, could not answer the purpose of a definition to others, to the unlearned at least; because the *definition is more obscure than the thing defined.* It contains a word, one of the most ambiguous in all Philosophy, the word *formal;*[p] and though most men have some idea of Logic, the great majority know nothing at all about *form*, except in the popular sense; so that to them the above definition would only be a bewilderment and a puzzle, rendering their previous conception not more clear, but more confused. Another able author, adopting this definition, explains *formal* to mean *necessary or essential;* so that according to him, Logic is the science of the Necessary Laws of Thoughts, and so he has entitled his Book. How then, it may be asked, is Logic distinguished from Metaphysics? Surely, Metaphysics treat of the necessary laws of thought, as well as of the laws of sensation and of emotion. Logic, then, is not a science distinct from Metaphysics, but only one part of it. Such a conclusion we can by no means admit, and therefore, the above definition must fall to the ground. But, if by the term *formal*, reference be made to words, and words be styled the *forms* of thoughts,

[p] For some account of the various senses in which the term *Form* has been used, see Thomson's "Outlines of the Necessary Laws of Thought." Introduction, section 5.

then, whether the above definition be full and adequate or not, it is at all events correct as far as it goes; for it points out one distinctive feature of Logic, namely, the alliance of thought with words. For Logic treats not of language merely, for then it would be Grammar; nor of thoughts only, for then it would be a branch of Metaphysics; but it treats of thoughts combined with words, or expressed in words. Thus, while letters, words, and sentences, belong to Grammar; conceptions, judgments, and reasonings, to Metaphysics; names, propositions, and arguments, are the subject of Logic.

Names suggest, or are meant to suggest things, whether material, as trees and stones, or immaterial, as sensations and conceptions; propositions express the relation of things; while arguments are propositions as inferred from other propositions.

According to this sense of the word *formal*, the definition of Sir William Hamilton would mean, that Logic is the science of the laws of thought in alliance with language. In this sense, I consider it correct, as far as it goes. Whether it be full and adequate is another question: as also, whether it be not too obscure for ordinary comprehension.

When Logic is styled the science of the

necessary laws of thought, there is a sense that might be given to the words which would exactly explain the object of one branch of the science, Logic proper or pure. Did these words imply, that the peculiar object of Logic was to teach us as much of the laws of thought as is necessary to maintain *consistency* in thinking, then the statement would be quite accurate. Consistency in thinking, as we shall see presently, is the especial object of simple Logic, not truth or agreement with the nature of things, which appertains to mixed or applied Logic. All the laws of thought belong not to Logic, but those only which maintain consistency in thinking. Thus Logic knows nothing of association, so important among the laws of thought.

Logic seems to hold a middle place between Metaphysics and Grammar. Metaphysics treat of the human mind and all its phenomena, which are comprised in three words, sensations, thoughts, and emotions; Logic treats only of thoughts combined with words, or expressed in words; while Grammar treats of words, all words, of which there are several sorts,—nouns, adjectives, verbs, adverbs, conjunctions, &c. Thus Logic agrees with Metaphysics, inasmuch as it treats of thoughts; but it differs in omitting sensations and emotions, and in treating of thoughts only in connection with words; while it agrees with Grammar in considering thoughts combined with words; but, whereas in Logic thought is the subject, and words are regarded only as subsidiary to thought; in Grammar, words are the subject, and thought is considered only as subsidiary to words, that is as necessary to determine that a word is truly a word, meaning something, and not a mere sound, or a mere number of letters thrown together, and also to fix of what sort any word may be, as noun, verb, or adverb.

The definition of Logic, as the science of the laws of thought in alliance with language, agrees with these views. But though accurate as far as it goes, in one respect at least it appears deficient, inasmuch as no allusion is made to Logic as a mixed science, combining speculation with practical application. On the contrary, by that definition, it would appear to be a science of pure speculation, like Metaphysics. But assuredly such is not Logic as generally understood. Whatever difference of views may be entertained as to the exact province of Logic, on one point, at least, almost all are agreed, namely, that Logic has a direct practical end in view, the improvement of our intellectual faculties, either in whole or in part. Now, though men *may* give any meaning to words they please, provided they explain their meaning, yet there is seldom any advantage in taking a well known word in a sense very different from the usual. At least, it ought to be done with great reserve. In the present instance, we see no sufficient reason for departing from the established meaning of the word *Logic*, and consequently we can by no means accept of the above definition as a full and adequate one, omitting, as it does, an essential element of the subject. At most, if Logic be divided into two parts, pure and mixed, that definition may suffice for the former, but it cannot embrace the whole.[q] We have, therefore, still to seek a full and adequate conception and definition of Logic; and for this purpose we must take a general survey of the mental sciences.

Those sciences, the subject of which is the human mind, may all be classed under one or

---

[q] Mr. De Morgan has written a treatise on Formal Logic, thereby implying that there is a Logic not formal; and Mr. Thomson, who considers Logic as the science of the necessary laws of thought, still divides it into pure and applied Logic. Saint Hilaire, in the preface to his translation of Aristotle's Organon, says, at one time, that Logic treats only of the form of thought; but he afterwards allows that there is such a thing as applied Logic, which treats of something else than form. Therefore, by his own showing, Logic, in its generic meaning, is not a mere science of form; pure Logic may be, but not *all* Logic; otherwise there is a contradiction.

other of the following heads:—I. Pure Mental Science. II. Mixed or Applied Mental Science. To the former, the term Metaphysics properly belongs, to the latter no common term is attached; but should we extend the meaning of the word Metaphysics, so as to comprise all mental science, then the one class would be pure, and the other mixed or applied Metaphysics. At present, however, for fear of ambiguity, we shall use Metaphysics in its more usual and restricted sense of pure mental science. This treats of the human mind, *as it is*, without any reference to direction and improvement. It is, therefore, purely speculative, and comprises :—I. The Analysis and Classification of the Mental Phenomena. II. The Theory of the origin and succession of the Mental Phenomena.[r]

The second class of the mental sciences is of a mixed nature, combining speculation with practical application. These sciences rest not in the knowledge of the human mind, as it is, but they have a further object, namely, to *direct* it, to direct thoughts, emotions, and through them, outward actions. This great class naturally divides itself into two, agreeably to

---

[r] As a specimen of Pure Mental Philosophy, I may be allowed to refer to my own "Analysis and Theory of the Emotions."

those two grand departments of the mind, THE UNDERSTANDING, and the EMOTIONS. To the latter, which has for its object to direct the Emotions in the pursuit of happiness, the term MORAL PHILOSOPHY may be applied, taken in the most extensive sense in which it can properly be used. In this sense, it includes not only Morals, strictly so called, or Ethics, but Politics in all its branches, as well as the science of Taste, of all which, the emotions of the human mind are the subject.

But what name belongs to the former branch of the mixed mental sciences, viz: that which professes to direct the understanding? Has it a name, or must we invent one? I confess that I see no occasion for a new term when an old one readily presents itself; and here the word LOGIC naturally occurs. This sense of the word may be very extensive, very vague if you will, but some word is required for this class of sciences, and whatever may be hit upon, the same objection may be made, which after all is no valid objection, for an extensive class must have a co-extensive name The only serious questions are two: are there sufficient grounds for the formation of a class of sciences, opposed to moral philosophy, and having for its object to direct the understanding, as the other has to direct or regulate the emotions; and if so, by what name shall we call it? Supposing that we adopt our known friend LOGIC, shall we be employing the term in an unwarrantable or very unusual sense? I think not. At least, the great father of modern philosophy, the immortal Bacon, has employed it in a sense no less extensive, for in his glorious work, the *De Augmentis*, he divides all the sciences which treat of the *uses* and *objects* of the mental faculties, into the two great classes of Logic and Ethics. The former of these he subdivides into the arts of discovering, judging, retaining, and communicating truth. Here, then, we have the word Logic used in a sense as extensive as that which I propose. Supported by so great an authority, I shall not scruple to define Logic, taken in its most comprehensive sense, as *the science which directs the understanding in the pursuit of Truth.*

Thoughts, then, are the subject of Logic, Truth the Object.

II. It must be allowed that Logic, as thus defined, comprehends a great deal, and, therefore, it will probably admit of several subdivisions. In tracing these subdivisions, we shall best discover what it comprises.

We must observe, in the first instance, that there is a branch of philosophy which seems to occupy a middle place between Metaphysics and

Logic, comprising, as it does, the first principles of human knowledge, principles, some of them strictly self-evident, others not strictly self-evident, nor yet capable of proof, which, nevertheless, must be taken for granted before we can advance one step. Of the first kind, are the axioms of mathematics, such as, things which are equal to the same thing are equal to one another; two straight lines cannot enclose a space; all right angles are equal to one another, &c. Of the second kind, are the following articles of belief:—

1. Belief in our own personal identity.
2. Belief in the faithfulness of memory; or in other words, trust in memory.
3. Belief in the existence of the external world.
4. Belief in the uniformity of nature.

Now, there is a branch of philosophy which has for its object to determine what are, and what are not, first principles, and on what ground they must be received. This, as I have observed, seems to hold a middle place between Metaphysics and Logic; but it belongs rather to the latter. If treated speculatively, as a matter of mere curiosity, it may be a branch of Metaphysics; but, in such a case, pure speculation without reference to application is hardly possible; and as the solidity of all our subsequent knowledge must depend upon the goodness of the foundation, and nothing can be raised without a foundation, therefore, the science which treats of *first* principles must be closely connected with that which treats of *secondary* principles, and the *advancement* of knowledge. For these reasons, we shall divide Logic, in the first instance, into *Primary* and *Secondary* Logic; the former being entirely devoted to the settlement of first or fundamental principles of belief. This may be otherwise called *Philosophia prima*.

III. We come now to the subdivisions of Secondary Logic. This, to which, by many, the term *Logic* would be confined, may be divided into two parts, the one of which we shall call *pure*, the other *applied* Logic. But though in reference to the latter, the former may well be called pure, yet it is not strictly a pure or unmixed science, like Metaphysics; for Metaphysics treat only of the phenomena of the human mind, whereas pure Logic treats of the phenomena of thought in connection with words. Moreover, as we shall see presently, even pure Logic has a direct practical object, which Metaphysics have not. It is called by some *Formal* Logic, words being considered as the forms of thought.

Pure or formal Logic is usually divided into three parts, which treat respectively, not of pure conceptions, judgments, and reasonings, as Metaphysics would treat, but of these united to words, that is, of names, propositions, and arguments. The former then are Metaphysical, the latter Logical terms. Pure Logic considers not how far names and the conceptions they raise correspond with the reality of things, nor yet whether propositions be true or false, nor even whether the conclusion of any argument be sound: but it determines what a name in general is, and what different sorts of names there may be, as singular or proper, and common or general, generic and specific, abstract and concrete; it analyzes a proposition, and shows of what parts all propositions are composed, and it also enumerates various kinds of propositions, such as categorical and hypothetical, affirmative and negative, universal and particular; and lastly, it analyzes the process of reasoning, points out different species thereof, and shows in what cases the conclusion does, and in what cases it does not follow from the premises, either demonstratively or probably. Thus the name *Centaur* answers to nothing in nature, but we have a conception thereof; the proposition, *Agamemnon slew Hector*, is false, but still, as a proposition, correct; the reasoning, *the mind of man is material, therefore, like other matter, it will enter after death into other combinations, and perish, as mind,* is correct, for the conclusion is fairly drawn, though it be false, because the premises are false. The words *true* and *false,* as applied to propositions and conclusions, do not belong to pure Logic; and instead thereof, we have *correct* and *incorrect, consistent, inconsistent,* and *contradictory.* Neither do the words *real* and *imaginary,* as applied to conceptions, appertain to Logic; instead of them, we have *clear* and *confused.*

According to the above view of the province of pure Logic, it may be defined as *the science which contains the rules of consistent thinking, as inferred from the verbal expression of thought.* Grammar, on the other hand, contains the rules of *correct expression,* as inferred from the common use of language.

Pure Logic and Grammar have both, then, a direct practical object, as implied by the word *rule;* the object of the one being *consistent thought,* of the other *correct expression.* Now, the rules of Grammar, though derived from the daily use of words, and liable to considerable varieties in different languages, have yet something common to all languages, and therefore, we may be sure, derived from the fundamental laws of thought. Consequently, there must be an intimate alliance between consistent thought and correct expression, between Logic and Grammar.

Both Logic and Grammar, as containing rules, partake of the nature of an art as well as a science. Pure Metaphysics, on the contrary, contains no rules, laws only; for it pretends not to direct, but simply to state what the mental phenomena are, to analyze and classify them, and to trace the general order of their succession.

IV. Applied Logic is opposed to pure, and forms the other part of secondary Logic. This is a much more comprehensive, as well as a less exact science than the former, for it applies the knowledge of the human mind and its processes, derived from Metaphysics and pure Logic, to the acquisition of objective truth, that is, the truth in all objects which the mind contemplates. Pure Logic contents itself with ascertaining that conceptions are clear, propositions correct, and not inconsistent with each other, and conclusions accurately drawn from premises; but applied Logic wishes to determine whether conceptions be agreeable to the reality of things, whether propositions and conclusions be true. Thus, the whole field of science is open to applied Logic, and consequently its scope is very extensive.

Though the sphere of applied Logic be so comprehensive, yet it does not seem to admit of any exact Logical division. But we can enumerate the principal subjects that fall within its province, which are as follows:—

1. A statement of the real object or objects of philosophy and science, and wherein these differ from other knowledge. Under this head, the words *cause* and *law of nature* must be explained.

2. A general account of the *means* whereby the sciences may be advanced, viz. experience, (including observation and experiments) and reasoning. Here the different sorts of reasoning must be mentioned, demonstrative and probable, inductive and deductive, and some general principles laid down, whereby it may be known what sort of reasoning is most applicable to any branch of science, and what degree of certitude it admits of. Here also an account should be given of the different methods used in scientific inquiry, such as the analytic and the synthetic. But the principal object of this department should be to trace the laws of induction, those of deduction belonging more particularly to pure Logic.*

3. An account of the various predisponent

---

* Mr. Mill has treated the subject of induction at length in his excellent work on Logic. The same subject had previously engaged Dr. Whewell in his great work, " the Philosophy of the Inductive Sciences."

causes of error or *idola* which beset the human mind.

4. An enquiry into the nature, use, and abuse of language, that great organ of human knowledge.

5. A general classification of the sciences, showing what sciences exist, how they are related, and pointing out new ones to the curiosity of mankind.

The first Book of Bacon's Novum Organum, and the fourth Book of Locke's Essay, may be taken as specimens of the art of attaining truth in general; while the second Book of the Organum contains special rules for induction; and the *De Augmentis Scientiarum* comprises a general classification of the objects of knowledge. The third Book of Locke, on the other hand, which treats of words, is for the most part a discourse on pure Logic, and perhaps the most valuable that ever was written on Names, the first division of the science. Indeed, the great work of Locke comprises pure Metaphysics, as well as Logic, in both its branches. The first and second Books, which treat of the mental phenomena, or ideas, as Locke calls them, their origin, nature, and succession, are purely Metaphysical; great part of the third Book, of Words, is pure Logic; and the fourth, of Knowledge and Opinion, is applied Logic.

Mr. Thomson, in his Outline of the Necessary Laws of Thought, has divided Logic into pure and applied, and has well pointed out the difference between them. The distinction is important. Formerly, as Mr. Thomson observes, applied Logic was treated of under the name of method, as a fourth branch of Logic in general; and classed along with the three branches of pure Logic.

The distinction here insisted on has been disregarded even by the best writers. Thus, Archbishop Whately considers all Logic as pure or formal, and makes no account of applied Logic. So does Sir W. Hamilton, who defines Logic to be the science of the formal laws of thought. Even Mr. Mill, in his great work, alludes not to this distinction. His division of the subject into ratiocinative and inductive Logic might seem indeed to point to it, were it not that under the former he treats of some things which do not belong to pure Logic. Watts makes a jumble of pure and applied Logic, for, after treating of Propositions logically, he has a chapter on Prejudices. Now, pure Logic treats indeed of *sophisms*, but knows nothing of the predisponent causes of error, *idola*, or prejudices. Even Bacon, in his *De Augmentis*, makes no distinction between pure and applied Logic.

Though the distinction between pure and mixed Logic be well founded on principle, yet we must not suppose that it is always easy to keep them separate in a logical treatise. The subject of Fallacies in particular shows how the one runs into the other. Though these have been distinguished into two sorts, fallacies *in Dictione,* and fallacies *extra Dictionem,* according as the sophism is supposed to lie in the *expression* or in the *matter,* yet there occur some which may be classed either with the one or with the other, or more properly with neither. These are when the middle term is ambiguous in *sense,* and they are called by Whately semi-logical fallacies.

V. Closely connected with applied Logic are the arts of retaining and communicating truth. These, indeed, have been classed by Bacon under the general name of Logic, and treated of accordingly;[t] but as this may be considered as too wide and vague a sense of the word, we prefer to consider these arts, not as integral parts, but as appendages of Logic.

Concerning the art of retaining truth, little need here be said. I shall observe only that it mainly depends upon three things,—ATTENTION REPETITION, and ASSOCIATION.

[t] See the De Augmentis Scientiarum, Lib. V. Cap. 1, and Lib. VI. Cap. 1.

In these three words nearly the whole art is comprised.

The art of communicating truth may be subdivided into three branches:—

1. The general art of Teaching.—2. Grammar.—3. Rhetoric.

It is proper, in a logical point of view, as well as highly useful, that the art of teaching should be considered as a separate special branch of knowledge, requiring a particular education, and not an art which any one may exercise who has acquirements, whether he have learnt how to communicate them or not. This is a principle which now seems recognised by the general adoption of training schools. We train schoolmasters for our village schools; but we have not yet begun to train them for schools of a higher order. If a man have taken a high degree at Oxford or Cambridge, if he be a good scholar, it is thought that he must needs be a good schoolmaster. A great mistake! The general art of teaching must give an account of the various modes as well as methods of teaching, their advantages and disadvantages: such as

1. Discourses written or unwritten, read or heard.

2. Questionings *viva voce*, or written: composing in prose or verse: learning by heart.

3. Ocular representations, such as pictures, maps, &c.

4. Experiments in mechanical philosophy and chemistry.

5. Dissections and demonstrations, as in anatomy.

6. Simple exhibitions of specimens, as in natural history.

Such are the *modes* of teaching. As for the *methods*, they are either public or private, solitary or simultaneous, magisterial or mutual; self-dependent for the most part, or dependent on assistance from others; between which last the difference is highly important.

We may also distinguish different *systems* of teaching; that for instance which tends to unity, simplicity, and concentration; and that which tends to multiplicity and diffusion; the former being the system of our ancestors, the latter that of the present day: the one calculated to make deeply learned and thoughtful students; the other to rear up imposing talkers and showy men of the world.

The second branch of the art of communicating truth is GRAMMAR, or the art of using language *correctly*; language being the grand organ of communication. Of the connection between pure Logic and Grammar, as well as of the difference between them, we have already spoken.

The third branch of the art of communicating, is RHETORIC, or the art of using language *effectively*, as Grammar is the art of using it *correctly*. Here we come to the very verge of our proper subject, if not beyond it; for the object of Logic and its attendant arts is simply truth; while that of Rhetoric is to render truth *effective*, that is acceptable or agreeable to those whom we address. Thus, Rhetoric speaks not only to the understanding, but also to the emotions, and therefore it really holds a middle place between Logic and Moral Philosophy.

To sum up all in a few words. The object of pure Logic is *consistency* in thought; of applied Logic, *truth*, or agreement of thought with the nature of things; of Grammar, *correctness* in language; of Rhetoric, *effect*.

# INTRODUCTION TO MENTAL PHILOSOPHY.

## PART SECOND.

#### COMPRISING:

I. THE CATEGORIES.
II. THE PROPOSITION.
III. REASONING.

Ce n'est pas *Barbara* et *Baralipton* qui forment le raisonnement. Il ne faut pas guinder l'esprit ; les manières tendues et pénibles le remplissent d'une sotte présomption par une élévation étrangère et par une enflure vaine et ridicule, au lieu d'une nourriture solide et vigoureuse.—Pascal.

# THE CATEGORIES.

Having completed our Philosophical Vocabulary, we are now better prepared for the consideration of the Categories. The term Categories, or rather the Categories, has been applied especially to the famous classification of Aristotle, under which he professed to include every object of human thought, every thing capable of being named. In other words, the Categories were the *Summa genera*, or highest classes, under which all things might be comprehended, all things of which we could think, or to which we could give a name. The Categories of Aristotle were the following:—

1. *Οὐσία*   Substance.
2. *Πόσον*   Quantity.
3. *Ποῖον*   Quality.
4. *Πρός τι* Relation.
5. *Ποῦ*     Where or Place.

6. Πότε    WHEN OR TIME.
7. Κεῖσθαί  SITUATION.
8. Ἔχειν    HAVING, HOLDING, OR POSSESSING.
9. Ποιεῖν   ACTION.
10. Πάσχειν PASSION.

Such is the celebrated classification of Aristotle; which, for the time when it appeared, may be considered as not unworthy of that great philosopher, though to us, at the present day, it appears very far from perfect, erring, as it does, by omission, as well as by redundancy.

First, as to omission. Among these Categories we look in vain for some things which have received names in all languages under the sun, things which are present to us during all our waking hours, and often even when asleep, which alone are intimately and immediately known to us, and by means of which alone we become acquainted with all other things. Such are the various sensations, thoughts, and emotions, which together make up our consciousness. Of these, which we may call in general mental phenomena, we find no mention in the above classification. Quality and Relation may no doubt apply to mind as well as to body; but sensations, emotions, and conceptions, are overlooked. This is the one great omission. The other faults are faults of redundancy.

Allowing that the first six genera are well distinguished, what can we think of classing Action and Passion as genera distinct from Relation? Both action and passion mean the relation of power, or of cause and effect, only with this difference, that action refers particularly to the cause or antecedent, passion to the effect or consequent; both being names of relation. Consequently, the ninth and tenth Categories must be expunged as redundant, being included under the fourth.

The fifth and sixth Categories, or Place and Time, are quite distinct; but how does Situation differ from Where or Place? Situation, Position, and Place, all mean the same thing; all relate to space, and to something existing in space, considered in reference to something else so existing. These somethings, being not named, must be supposed included under one of the other Categories, as Space is included under Place or *Where*. Consequently, the seventh Category may be expunged as redundant.

And surely the eighth, Having, Holding, or Possessing, can have no pretence to a *Summum genus*, expressing, as it does, not a simple thing, but something very complex, the elements of which must be comprehended under the other Categories. Therefore, the eighth Category may also be expunged.

Aristotle's chapter on the eighth Category, on Possession, is rather curious. It resembles more an article in a dictionary, giving the various senses of the Greek word Ἔχειν, than a chapter in a scientific work. Thus, we are told that Ἔχειν, to have, is variously used:—1. First, as a mode of being, a disposition or habit, as when we say that a man has science or virtue. 2. As quantity, for instance, the height we have. 3. As having what surrounds the body, a garment, a cloak. 4. Having in or on a part of the body, as having a ring on one's finger. 5. Or, in relation to a part of the body, as having a hand or a foot. 6. Containing any thing, as a cask has wine. 7. Possessing, as having land or houses. 8. Having, as a wife or a husband. There may be some faint analogy between all these significations, but none sufficient to establish a definite meaning of the word, fit for scientific purposes. Indeed this chapter is quite unworthy of Aristotle.[a]

From the above examination it appears that, of the ten Categories of Aristotle, four must be expunged as redundant; while one must be added to render the list complete. The amended classification will then be the following:—

1. MENTAL PHENOMENA.

[a] Categories, Chap. XV.

2. SUBSTANCE, divided into two species, Mind or Spirit, and Body or Matter.

3. QUANTITY.

4. QUALITY, also divided into two species, Mental Quality, and Bodily Quality.

5. RELATION.

6. PLACE, or more simply SPACE, Place involving a Relation.

7. TIME.

This new classification must be allowed to be an improvement upon the old; but we may farther inquire whether it may not be rendered still better. It is clear that if Space and Time be allowed to stand distinct from Quantity, then we must add to these Number, for otherwise it will not be included under any Category. Therefore, to the above seven Categories we shall add

8. NUMBER.

Two questions, however, still remain to be discussed: first, whether Time, Space, and Number should be classed distinct from Quantity; and secondly, whether Relation should be separated from Quality.

We have seen in the First Part, the Philosophical Vocabulary, that Quantity belongs not only to Material Substance, but to Time, Space, and Number, considered without any reference to Substance. With all these, Quantity is inseparably connected; that is, wherever Material Substance, Time, Space, or Number exists, there is Quantity. Still, Quantity does not necessarily suppose Substance, for there may be Quantity of Time or of pure Space; nor does Quantity necessarily suppose Time, for there may be Quantity of Space; nor does Quantity necessarily suppose Space, for there may be Quantity of Time or of Number; nor finally, does Quantity necessarily suppose Number, for there may be Quantity of Time or of Space. Therefore, Quantity is something which is neither Substance, nor Time, nor Space, nor Number, and therefore it is properly classed apart.

With respect to the second question, whether Relation should be classed apart from Quality, it may at first appear that such separation is incorrect, because we have seen in the former part, the Philosophical Vocabulary, that at bottom every Quality does suppose Relation of some kind or other. But at the same time we remarked, that there was a real difference between Qualities, commonly called Simple, and Relative Qualities, inasmuch as the Relation in the former case, though it may be discovered by Metaphysical analysis, is commonly not attended to, our thoughts being centered, sometimes on the cause, sometimes on the effect, not on the Relation between them. This is one reason why Relation should be classed apart from Quality; but there is another more satisfactory.

Though, strictly speaking, there is no Quality without some Relation, yet, in the case of Quantity, there is Relation without Quality. The Relations of Quantity in Space, Time, and Number, are the subject of pure Mathematics; the Relations of Quantity in Body, of mixed Mathematics; and these are quite distinct from Quality. Therefore Quality and Relation ought not to be classed together.[b]

Some there are who class Quality, Relation, and Quantity, all together, under the common name Attribute; but this classification must be purely verbal, unless it can be shown wherein these three agree; and for my own part I can see no agreement, nor do I find that Logicians have been able to define Attribute so taken. Mr. Mill allows that Logicians have not given any satisfactory account of Attribute when taken to comprehend

---

[b] The difficulty of distinguishing between Quality and Relation was well seen by Aristotle; for after some discussion on the subject, he ends by saying "After all, if the same thing may be at the same time a Relation and a Quality, there is nothing absurd in classing it under both genera."—*Categories, Chap. VIII.*—In this case there certainly would be a Logical imperfection, for no one genus should over-lay another.

Quality, Relation, and Quantity. (System of Logic Book I. Chap. iii. s. 6.) Another Author, and one of very high authority, classes Quantity, Quality, and Relation, under the common head *Ens per accidens*, in opposition to *Ens per se* or Substance; but I do not see that *Ens per accidens* admits of any better definition than Attribute.[c]

Attribute is generally supposed to belong to Substance, and to be inseparable from it, as when we talk of a Substance and its Attributes; but then, Quantity is not an Attribute, for Space, Time, and Number have Quantity, though they are not Substances. So Space, Time, and Number, have Relations quite independent of Substance, which Relations cannot therefore be Attributes. Therefore, in the vocabulary, I have restricted Attribute to the sense of Quality alone, and more particularly to one species of Quality.[d]

Moreover, the word attribute is liable to ambiguity, for it has two senses, a Metaphysical and a Logical. When we divide things into Substances and Attributes, it is clear that we speak metaphysically; and the division is incomplete, for Time, Space, and Number, are not Substances, nor Attributes of Substances. But when we talk

[c] See notes to Reid's Brief account of Aristotle's Logic, p. 688 of Reid's works, edited by Sir William Hamilton.

[d] See article QUALITY.

of Subject and Attribute, then we speak Logically, and Attribute becomes synonymous with Predicate: whereas in the former sense it corresponded to Quality or Property. To avoid this ambiguity, the word *Accident*, or *Ens per accidens*, has been substituted for Attribute, in the metaphysical sense.

Upon the whole, until a better division be pointed out, I must be satisfied with the eight Categories given above, for I cannot see that they err either by omission or by redundancy. It appears to me that all the objects of thought, all that may become the subject of science, can be classed under one or other of these Categories. But in order fully to ascertain this point, let us consider first our various mental Phenomena, and their Objects, and secondly the various Sciences.

Since the above professes to be a complete enumeration of the elementary objects of thought, there should be a thought, or, in the language of Locke, a simple idea, corresponding to each of these objects, and to none besides, while all other or complex ideas should be made up of these simple ones. This is only to say that thoughts and the objects of thoughts must correspond. Let us then see whether the former do tally with the enumeration above given of the latter.

All the Phenomena of Mind may be divided into two great Classes, the one of which may be called the Class of Outward, the other that of Inward Phenomena; not that the former are less mental than the latter, but that it is by those alone we become acquainted with the world without. Outward Phenomena may be divided into two genera, Sensations and Perceptions. Inward Phenomena are divided into two orders, Intellectual Phenomena, or Thoughts, and Emotions, which are distinguished from each other by the absence or presence of *Feeling*, in the strict sense of the word, that is of Pleasure or Pain, Happiness or Misery. Thoughts, again, are subdivided into Conceptions and Relations, according as they do not, or do, necessarily suppose two things compared together. Conceptions are either simple or compound, the latter comprehending conceptions of Substances and their qualities, and conceptions of Modes, or modifications of things independent of Substance; while Relations are either of co-existence, of succession, or of resemblance. Such, in short, is a classification of the Mental Phenomena, made without any reference to the above classification of Things or Categories, the same in fact which appeared some years ago in my Principles of Human Happiness, and differing little from that of the late Dr. Brown. Let us then see whether the two classifications agree.

To begin with the Phenomena of Mind generally; these find a place, the first place in the Categories. It is clear that the Phenomena of Mind may themselves be objects of Thought.

Sensations, in the strict sense of the word, have no Objects, we are conscious of them, and that is all; for they do not suggest their causes directly, but indirectly, through our perceptions. Now the objects of our Perceptions are the Qualities of Matter, and these find a place among the Categories. Among the Inward Phenomena, Emotions, like Sensations, are felt, as pleasurable or painful, but they also have no proper objects; for what are called objects of desire are known to us not by our Emotions, but by our perceptions or conceptions, which inform us of things suited to rouse Emotion. The other order of Inward Phenomena is that of Thoughts, divided into Conceptions and Relations. These last are also among the Categories. They are divided into Relations of co-existence, of succession, and of resemblance, a classification which holds good, as we have seen, whether Relation be taken in the restricted sense of a Mental Phenomenon looking to two other mental phenomena, or generally, of something common to two other things. Now, of the Relations of co-existence, some necessarily suppose Space, as Relations of Position; others Number, as the Rules of Arithmetic; and both of these Quantity; while Relations of Succession necessarily suppose Time. But Space, Number, Time, and Quantity, are among the Categories.

Lastly, Conceptions are either simple or compound. Our knowledge of the former is obtained by analyzing the latter, which are divided into Conceptions of Substances, with their Qualities, and what I call Conceptions of Modes, or modifications of things which do not necessarily suppose Substance, namely, of Space, Time, and Number. From the conceptions of individual Substances, and different species of Substances, with their respective qualities, we rise to the conception of Substance in general, which alone remained to complete our eight Categories.

Thus it appears that all the eight Categories, and as far as we can see, no others, have Mental Phenomena corresponding to them, Phenomena of which those are the Objects; and if so, the correctness of the above enumeration of Categories is confirmed.

Let us now compare the various Sciences with the Categories above given. For this purpose I shall take that Classification of the Sciences which I published some time ago, and which had engaged my attention for years, long before I thought of these Categories. According to that Classification, the Sciences are divided into the Mental, the Physical, and the Mathematical, or Metaphysics, Physics, and Mathematics. The Mental Sciences treat either of the Substance Mind, or of its Qualities, Relations, and Phenomena, all of which are included in the Categories; while the Physical Sciences treat of the Substance Body, its Qualities and Relations, which also are contained in the same. Lastly, Mathematics treat of Quantity, whether of Space, Time, or Number, and these make up the rest of the Categories.

The Book of Categories, divided into fifteen chapters, forms the first part of Aristotle's great Work on Logic—The Organon. Notwithstanding, an eminent Logician of the present day, and at the same time a great admirer of Aristotle, maintains that the doctrine of the Categories belongs not to pure Logic, because it treats of THINGS. It cannot be denied, however, that the doctrine of NAMES appertains to pure Logic, and if so, the classification of names. Therefore the Categories of Names, at least, belong to pure Logic. But the Categories of Names are the same as the Categories of Things, and in classifying the one, we classify the other also. A Name without a thing corresponding to it, is a contradiction. Mere Articulate sounds, expressed by letters and syllables, such as *Fanfarom*, are not Names, for they stand for no Thing. Consequently the Categories *do* belong to pure Logic.

Indeed, the doctrine of the Categories belongs to that branch of Philosophy which I have called *Philosophia prima*, as well as to pure Logic. It is the connecting link between them. *Philosophia prima*, or Primary Logic, treats, as we have seen, of the first Principles of human knowledge, the fundamental Principles of belief; and it must also include the Elements of all knowledge, the Categories of things. Pure Logic, on the other hand, begins with Names, and in classifying them classifies Things also. Thus the two Sciences meet.

# PROPOSITION, THE PREDICABLES.

The doctrine respecting Proposition has been involved in some obscurity, from a want of attention to three fundamental distinctions; for there are three important questions which ought to be discussed separately. The first, what is a Proposition? What is the definition of a Proposition in general?

I. A Proposition may be considered under two points of view. We may look more particularly to the mind which frames it, or else to the form of words in which it is expressed. For every Proposition supposes a mental act, and a verbal expression. Or what comes to the same thing, we may attend chiefly to the mental operation necessary to a Proposition, or else to the formal result. The first belongs to the province of the pure Metaphysician, the second, to that of the Logician and Grammarian. It appertains then to pure Metaphysics to determine the nature of those faculties necessary to form a Proposition; while to Logic, and Grammar, belongs the result, viz. the Proposition itself. Now, as Conception and Judgment are universally allowed to be indispensable to the framing of any Proposition, and as the latter of these faculties supposes the former, as, moreover, there is no Proposition without words, it follows that, metaphysically, a Proposition may be defined *a judgment expressed in words.*

This, though a correct metaphysical definition, will not be of any use until judgment itself be defined; and therefore we must adopt another method of ascertaining the nature of a Proposition. While the Metaphysician analyzes the phenomena of mind in order to determine the nature of judgment, the Logician must analyze Propositions themselves. As examples take the following :—

1. Man is mortal.
2. The Elephant is long lived.
3. The Lion is carnivorous.
4. The Hare is timid.
5. Courage is admired.
6. Virtue is esteemed.
7. Generosity is beloved.
8. Deer are not carnivorous.
9. Cowardice is not respected.

10. Napoleon was not a saint.

11. Washington was not an usurper.

12. Brutus killed Cæsar.

13. Antony loved Cleopatra.

14. Alexander conquered Darius.

15. The three angles of a triangle are equal to two right lines.

16. Any two sides of a triangle are together greater than the third side.

17. The French Convention treated Louis XVI. cruelly.

18. The Chamber of Peers condemned Ney to death ungenerously.

19. Italy may be free.

20. No one can say.

21. Napoleon might have conquered Russia.

All these, however different, will be universally allowed to be Propositions, and if so, there must be something common to them all.

In the first place, they are all composed of words, and of words which, taken together, make perfect sense, one of them being a verb. In short, they are all sentences. But, there are sentences, such as a question, a prayer, a command, which are not Propositions. Secondly, each of these Propositions has two extremes or terms, as they are called, such as Man and Mortal, Generosity and Beloved, Brutus and Killed Cæsar, three angles of a triangle and equal to two right angles, &c., one of which is called the Subject, the other the Predicate. Thirdly, these two terms are connected by means of a verb, which is sometimes the simple copula or sign of affirmation *is*, at other times a word of a more compound signification, such as *killed, loved, conquered*, which involves an affirmation, and may be analyzed into *was the killer of, was the lover of, was the conqueror of.* Sometimes to the verb is added the sign of denial *not*; sometimes other words which modify the sense, such as *equal to*, and *greater than, cruelly, ungenerously;* or some modification of the verb is used, as *may be, can say*, or *might have.* From all this it follows that a Proposition may be defined to be *a sentence, or combination of words with meaning, whereby something is affirmed or denied of some other thing, either simply, or with some modification.*

This is the proper Logical definition of a Proposition; the Metaphysical definition of the same being as above stated, *a judgment expressed in words.*

The Logical definition might be expressed more shortly, but rather obscurely, as *a sentence declaratory or enunciative.* Different modes of declaration are called in Grammar, MOODS, as the Indicative, Subjunctive, Potential, Optative. The close connection between Logic and Grammar everywhere appears.

From the above we see that every Proposition must have two terms at least. But there are sentences which all allow to be Propositions, though they *seem* to have only one term, such as it rains, it snows, it thunders, and God is, the Lion exists, &c. With respect to the first class of these, we may observe that the indefinite word *it* refers to some subject or other understood, though it does not at once appear to what subject, whether sky, cloud, or air. The pronoun *it* came to be used, either for brevity, or because the proper subject was doubtful, but it evidently points to something; and the phrase, it rains, is exactly equivalent to the sky rains, or the cloud, or the air rains. Again the word *rains* is an abbreviation of *is raining*, and the one may be substituted for the other, without the least inaccuracy. Therefore, at full, the sentence *it rains* becomes, *the air, or sky, or cloud is raining*, which is a Proposition in due form.

As to the second class of Propositions, apparently incomplete, God is, the Lion exists, &c., we must remember that the word *is* has two distinct meanings. Sometimes it is a mere copula, the sign of affirmation, connecting the Predicate with the Subject, as when we say a triangle is a three sided figure; but at other times it comprehends besides this the notion of real existence. Thus, the sentence *God is*, means *God exists*, or at full, *God is existing*, which is a regular Proposition. In like manner, *the Lion exists*, is equivalent to *the Lion is existing*; and so with all other Propositions of the sort in which real existence is predicated of something, whether by means of the verb *to be*, or of the less ambiguous verb *to exist*.

As there are some Propositions which seem to contain less than two terms, so are there others, or Compound Propositions, which contain more than two; but these can all be resolved into simple ones. Thus, the compound proposition, *Brutus and Cassius waged war with Octavius and Antony*, comprehends the following simple propositions:—

      Brutus waged war with Octavius.
      Brutus waged war with Antony.
      Cassius waged war with Octavius.
      Cassius waged war with Antony.

Those two together waged war with these two together.

This example may suffice to show how Compound Propositions may be analyzed. Here we see that the first particle *and* replaces one entire proposition, the second *and* two propositions, the two taken together one more; so that this one compound proposition contains five simple.

II. Having determined the nature of a Proposition, and having seen that it is always composed of two terms at least, connected together by an affirmative or negative copula, the second principal question presents itself, viz. What things may be signified by those terms?

Now, whatever may be of itself an object of Thought, and as such can receive a fully significant name, may be the subject or predicate of a Proposition; for of such an object something or other may be affirmed or denied, or that object may itself be affirmed or denied of something else. Therefore, the terms of all Propositions must correspond to one or other of the Categories of Things, which we have already determined.

With reference to Things compared, there must then be at least as many sorts of Propositions, as there are Categories. Thus, we may have Propositions where Mental Phenomena are compared with Mental Phenomena, Spirit with Spirit, Body with Body, Quality with Quality, Relation with Relation, Quantity with Quantity, Space with Space, Time with Time, and Number with Number.

This only we must remember, that, while the

subject of a Proposition may be either a general or a singular Name, as, Man is a religious being; Socrates was a Moral Philosopher; the predicate must be general, for predication means that something common to many things is affirmed or denied of one or more. No proposition then can exist without a general term. We can make no proposition out of proper names alone, but only the unmeaning form of, Socrates is, or was, not Solon.

When we consider attentively these various sorts of Propositions, we shall find, however, that they may be reduced to a smaller number. All Propositions relative to Mind and its Phenomena may be properly considered as forming but one class, that of Mental Propositions; all relative to Body, its qualities and relations, another, under the name of Physical Propositions; while those which relate to Quantity, whether of Space, Time, or Number, may be called Mathematical Propositions; a classification exactly corresponding to that of the Sciences.

According to this view, the above eight Categories might be reduced to three, Mind, Body, Quantity, under one or other of which all things might be comprehended. In this view, under the term Mind, would be comprised not only the permanent thing, or substance, Spirit, but also its qualities, and its fugitive phenomena; under Body, not only the substance Body, but all its qualities and relations; while all the relations of Space, Time, and Number, would be comprehended under Quantity.

But whether we adopt this classification of Categories or not, as preferable to that before given, the division of Propositions into Mental, Physical, and Mathematical, seems agreeable to the nature of things, as well as to the natural division of the Sciences, which are made up of Propositions, and of nothing else. Other Propositions, no doubt, there are, of a mixed nature, such as all those relative to the influence of Mind on Body, or of Body on Mind; where the things are widely different, though there be a relation between them. These may be called mixed Propositions, the terms corresponding to things belonging to different Categories.

We see from the above the futility of those discussions which have so much occupied Logicians, respecting the terms of a Proposition, whether they correspond to Ideas, to Things, or to Names. Some Propositions, it is clear, relate to Ideas, others to things different from Ideas. In the proposition, "ambition is a more durable passion than love," it is quite evident that the terms Ambition and Love stand for Emotions, which are Feelings, or Mental Phenomena. But in the proposition, "gold is heavier than lead," it is no less evident that the terms gold and lead stand for material substances, which all mankind believe, whether with or without reason, to have an independent existence without the mind. True it is that gold and lead are known to us only through our Sensations and Perceptions, and that we can form no Proposition respecting them, but through the notions of our mind. But, the common observer, as well as the physical enquirer, does not stop to analyze the notion, as the Metaphysician does, but he passes on at once to the material object; of that he thinks, concerning that he forms an opinion, and makes a proposition. Can any one really maintain that there is no difference in the terms of the two propositions above stated, that gold and lead, no less than love and ambition, stand for Ideas or Mental Phenomena, and nothing else? Surely common sense is sufficient to settle this question. Without entering upon the grounds of our conviction, it is certain that, in speaking of gold and silver, we speak of things which we believe to be distinct from the mind and its phenomena.

One very celebrated Metaphysician[e] has maintained that in all Propositions the terms of com-

[e] Hobbes.

parison are Names, and nothing but Names. Let us examine the meaning of this statement, and see how it applies. To suppose that in the Proposition, "ambition is a more durable passion than love," all we assert is that the name ambition is more durable than the name love, is an absurdity too palpable to be maintained by any one. Do we then compare the meaning of the names, and do we assert that the meaning of the name ambition is more durable than the meaning of the name love? This also is an absurdity. We must assert then that the name ambition means something which is more durable than what is meant by the name love. The question then comes to be, do we here assert that the name ambition, in the proper, that is in the usual signification of words, implies a passion more durable than love, as a part of its definition? or, do we assert a new fact not supposed to be included in the common sense of the word? If the former, then our Proposition is one relating to the meaning of a word, or verbal; if the latter, then our Proposition is real, where one thing is compared with another thing, not a name with a meaning or thing. For this is a verbal Proposition, where the two terms are a name, a mere name, and a thing; and the assertion is that the one is, or is not, generally employed to mean the other. To which of these kinds of Propositions, "ambition is more durable than love" belongs, the reader will at once determine; and if this be a real Proposition, then all Propositions are not verbal.

Though all Propositions be not verbal, yet some are. A verbal Proposition, as we have said, is one where one of the terms is a mere Name, and the other a Name or Names suggesting a Thing; so that even in verbal Propositions one of the terms is a Thing. Thus, in the verbal Proposition, " a triangle is a figure with three sides and three angles," the assertion is that the word *triangle*, either in ordinary discourse, or else in books of Science, means the thing here described. The word triangle may be supposed to convey no meaning at all before one meets with this Proposition; it is a collection of letters, an articulate sound, but it may be nothing else. This Proposition makes it a true word, that is, gives it a meaning which it had not before, states a Thing to which by convention it is applicable. Such is a verbal Proposition.

Though some verbal Propositions are altogether trifling, the bane of science, and the source of endless and unprofitable disputes, because they are not at once seen to be verbal; yet we must not suppose that all verbal Propositions are vain and futile. On the contrary, some of the most important Propositions are strictly verbal. Such are all definitions. The object of a definition, such as that of a triangle above given, is to give a meaning, a definite meaning, to a word before supposed either to have none, or one uncertain and fluctuating. Consequently, a Name, a mere Name, is one term of the Proposition, and a Name or Names which stand for Things is another. Now, in order to determine to what Things a Name should be applicable, we must have clear notions of the nature of Things, their resemblances, and differences; for to things similar we give a common name, to things different, different names. Therefore, a good definition often requires a long and painful investigation into the nature of Things, and ought to be not the beginning but the end of our inquiries, the summing up of all that we have learnt. Thus, it appears that definitions, though verbal Propositions, are not inferior in importance to real.

Some verbal Propositions are evidently so, but not all. Where one of the Names is a new word suggesting nothing, then any assertion concerning it must be seen to be verbal; but where both are old and well known, we are apt to think that neither requires definition, and therefore that whatever is said of one of them must be a fact not referring to the meaning of the Name.

Since verbal Propositions are so insidious, it becomes very desirable to have some ready criterion, whereby we may discover them. As one criterion, I may mention the employment of a definition. If a dispute be at once terminated by a definition, then we may be sure that the Proposition contested is purely verbal. Suppose the question to be, whether Prudence be a virtue. Define Virtue, and the dispute is settled at once; therefore the question is verbal.

I may suggest another criterion. Since the simple copula *is* is alone employed in definition, and alone necessary, wherever we find a Proposition containing that copula as the only verb, there we should be on our guard. Substitute for the verb *is*, the word *means*, or the words *means something comprehended under the meaning of*, and if the Proposition then make sense, we may be sure that it is verbal.

Thus, in the Proposition, "a triangle is a figure with three sides and three angles," substitute *means* for *is*, and the sense is the same. So in the Proposition "prudence is a virtue," substitute the other phrase, and we have "prudence means something comprehended under the meaning of virtue," which is also sense. Both these then are verbal Propositions. But substitute either of these phrases in the Proposition, "ambition is a more durable passion than love," and the result is nonsense. This, therefore, is not a verbal Proposition. Ambition may be a more durable passion than love, but certainly that is not the meaning of the word ambition.

Wherever the Predicate contains the whole of the definition, there the copula *is* or *means* is employed; but where it contains only a part of the definition, there the longer form of words must be used. Thus in the Proposition, "a triangle is, or means, a figure with three sides, and three angles," the Predicate is a complete definition; while in this, "prudence is a virtue, i. e. means something comprehended under the meaning of virtue," the predicate is only a part of the definition, the genus, of which prudence is a species.

We must here observe that the distinctions of Propositions into Mental, Physical, and Mathematical, into real and verbal, are Metaphysical, not Logical distinctions; for they relate to the nature of Things which the terms stand for; whereas pure Logic looks only to the Form or Expression. Thus, in pure Logic, Propositions are divided into Categorical, and Hypothetical, according as they enounce absolutely, or under a condition; as, "man is a rational animal," is Categorical; "the boy may learn," Hypothetical. Propositions are again divided, in pure Logic, into Affirmative and Negative, Universal and Particular, words which explain themselves. These distinctions need not here be dwelt upon, as they are found in all books of Logic: but what is necessary to attend to, is the difference between the Logical and the Metaphysical nature of Propositions. It is the latter of these that I here treat of.

It was necessary in the first instance to determine the nature of a Proposition, both Metaphysically, and Logically, and to define it accordingly: but the rest of this article relates to Propositions considered Metaphysically. The Logical divisions of Propositions, and the Logical Predicables also, as we shall see presently, must not be confounded with the Metaphysical divisions and the Metaphysical Predicables.

Here it may not be out of place to remark, once for all, that the word *Metaphysical* is used in three different senses at least, which may be determined by the context. We shall know the meaning of the word, by considering to what it is opposed. When Metaphysical is opposed to Physical or Material, it means Mental. In this sense, Metaphysics is sometimes called Psychology. But when Metaphysical is opposed to Logical, then, as, on the one hand, Logical refers to *consistent thinking*, Metaphysical, on the other, relates to the correspondence between our thoughts and the nature of things. In this sense, Metaphysical and Real are synonymous. Logical truth is sometimes called *subjective*, as confined to the subject who thinks, and Metaphysical *objective*, as relating to an object, either really distinct, or considered for the time as distinct from the subject. Lastly, Metaphysical sometimes means nothing more than *exact*, and Metaphysically true is exactly true. Thus, Mr. James Mill, in his Elements of Political Economy, says, "the objection is not only practically immaterial, it is metaphysically unsound."

III. Having determined the nature of a Proposition in general, and also having seen what the two terms of a Proposition stand for, what things they are meant to represent; it now remains in the third place, to ascertain what it is which we affirm or deny concerning these things. This is the doctrine of Predication, or of the Predicables, as it is commonly called in books of Logic, an acquaintance with which will complete what is here necessary to be known with respect to Propositions. We have seen that in every Proposition there are at least two terms, and that the thing suggested by one of these terms is affirmed or denied of the thing suggested by the other. But this we cannot do with meaning, unless we see that there is, or is not some relation between them. The feeling of relation is distinguished from conception by this, that it necessarily implies three mental states, two conceptions, and the relative feeling which connects them. So, the objects which correspond to those conceptions are considered, either each alone and separate, or else as bearing one upon the other, as somehow connected, or related. Now what a Proposition sets forth in words is, that such and such a relation does or does not subsist between two things which are named. In short, there are two things, and not one alone mentioned, and an assertion is made concerning these two things, that they have or have not something in common. Consequently, what is asserted, or predicated, is a relation.

This being determined, our task may be considered as nearly accomplished, for we have already considered the subject of relation, and the various kinds thereof. Relations, we have seen, are either of Coexistence, of Succession, or of Resemblance, and consequently, if Predication mean the affirmation or denial of a relation, then, in every Proposition, what we affirm or deny is, that some coexistence, or some succession, or some resemblance, subsists between two things. Such is the nature of Predication; and these are three Predicables.

Are these then the only Predicables? If all propositions contained two terms respecting two things really different, and not one and the same, then every affirmation or denial concerning them would be the predication of some Relation, which would be one either of coexistence, of succession, or of resemblance. But there are some propositions, regular in form and real as to matter, in which the two terms stand for one and the same thing. When I say, "this is the man whom I met yesterday," I state two propositions, both regular, and taken together instructive; though the terms of the first stand for the same thing, the same individual man. But between an individual and the same individual there cannot be, properly speaking, any Relation, for relation supposes two things and not one only. Therefore, to meet such cases as this, we must allow another Predicable, distinct from those above mentioned, viz. that of Identity, or Sameness; meaning by this, real sameness, and not merely close resemblance, as the word often signifies. Propositions predicating identity may no doubt be verbal, but they are not so necessarily. When I say, "this is the man who won the prize," the proposition, or rather the propositions, are real; but when I state that "Setubal and Saint Ubes are the same," what I affirm is that the proper names, Setubal and Saint Ubes denote the same place, an affirmation evidently verbal.

We must not confound propositions predicating identity with those which have been called identical propositions; such as "a square is a square," "a man is a man," "an elephant is an elephant," wherein a term is affirmed of itself. These are the very perfection of trifling, for they give us no information, even as to the meaning of names. But it is unnecessary to add one word to what Locke has written on these frivolous propositions.

There is still another sort of propositions, where we look in vain for any proper relation between two things. This is the case where existence alone is predicated. "God is," is assuredly a proposition, and one of vast importance, though in form it be so simple; it is, as we have seen, equivalent to "God exists," or "is existing," or "is an existing Being;" a proposition, in which it is not easy to trace any coexistence, succession, or resemblance. If "God is" were equivalent to "God is one of existing beings", then it might be said that the proposition stated a resemblance between God and other beings, a resemblance in their common existence, though this would be farfetched; but "God is," does not seem to refer to any other being; it is, as far as possible, an absolute Proposition. Therefore, to those Predicables before mentioned we must now add that of Existence. The complete list of the Predicables will then be, RELATION, whether of *Coexistence, Succession,* or *Resemblance,* IDENTITY, EXISTENCE.

Is it possible to explain what we mean by Existence, or is our notion thereof too simple to admit of analysis? With the word *Existence* is often joined the word *Real,* as if Real Existence were different from Existence simply. Real Existence then may admit of analysis, though Existence do not. By Real Existence, I conceive we mean Substantial Existence, Existence as a substance, that is, as something permanent among innumerable modifications. Now substances are of two sorts, Spirit and Body; and therefore Real Existence means Existence as a Spirit or as a Body.

Simple Existence seems to me to defy analysis. Many things are allowed to exist which have no Real or Substantial Existence, such as the thoughts which flit across our mind. Even Time and Space are said to exist; though, wherein empty space differs from nothing no one can tell; and if time and space exist, then do their modifications exist, and the figures of Mathematics exist, though not bodily. On the other hand, we can conceive things which no one now allows to exist, as centaur, mermaid, land unicorn.

These are said to exist only in idea or in imagination; that is, the idea exists, but nothing corresponding thereto, absolutely nothing. But when we say that mathematical triangles and squares do not exist, all we mean is, that they do not exist bodily; we allow that they exist somehow, though how we cannot tell; we do not look upon them as chimeras, centaurs, and unicorns, which have no sort of existence.

When existence is predicated of any thing, *real* existence is almost always meant. Thus "God is," means, God exists as a substantial or permanent Being, endowed with innumerable attributes. The question whether time and space exist, may be regarded as, at bottom, but verbal, or a question as to the applicability of the word *exists;* though, like many other verbal disputes, it touches hard upon things. For if, by denying that space and time, and the figures of Mathematics, exist, we are led to infer that the science of Mathematics has no base, a question that might seem but verbal, becomes raised to one of real importance.

These, then, we propose as a list of the Predicables, of all that can be affirmed or denied of any thing. When we affirm that "the wild rose has five petals," we state a Relation of Co-existence; when we say "opium causes sleep," we bring forward a Relation of Succession, in this case, of Cause and Effect; when we assert that "a bat is like a bird," or that "blue is like green," we enounce a Relation of Resemblance; when we say " this is the same man who kept the inn ten years ago," we declare Identity; and lastly, when we conclude from the innumerable proofs of design in the universe, that "there is a God," we proclaim His real existence.

2. I shall conclude this subject with a few remarks on some former lists of Predicables. The most ancient, and the most celebrated of these, is contained in "Prophyry's Introduction to the Categories," which for many ages was adopted by Logicians as the standard work on this subject, adopted as of equal authority with the Organon of Aristotle, to which it was prefixed. According to this famous classification, all that could be predicated of any thing was, its

  GENUS,
  SPECIES,
  SPECIFIC DIFFERENCE, or DIFFERENTIA,
Some PROPERTY,
Or some ACCIDENT of the same.

When I say, "a triangle is a figure," I predicate the Genus to which triangle belongs; when I state, "a triangle is a figure with three sides and three angles," I enounce the Species;

when I affirm, "a triangle has three sides and three angles," I mention the Difference which distinguishes it from other species of the same genus, Figure; when I declare that "in every triangle any two of the sides are together greater than the third side," I assert a Property; and when I observe, "this triangle is large," I state an Accident.

Now what first strikes us with respect to this famous classification, is, that three of these Predicables are applicable only to verbal Propositions, i. e. to Propositions concerning the signification of names. The first three are all about definition, and nothing else. In saying that a triangle is a figure, I so far define a triangle as to distinguish it from a host of other things which are not figures, and in stating farther that it is a figure with three sides and three angles, I complete the definition by mentioning how it differs from other figures. But in all this, the question is merely as to the meaning of the word *triangle*, as to what it is used to represent. So when I say that a man is an animal, or a rational animal, I state only what the name *man* generally means, what it is supposed usually to suggest; I affirm nothing more. In short, the Genus is a part of the definition, the Specific difference is the other part, and the two together make up the complete definition of the Species, so that one and all give only the meaning of names, and their place in the scale of classification as Genus or Species. Therefore, these three ought to be excluded from a list of *real* Predicables, whereby some information is afforded not comprised in the received signification of a name. In opposition to the latter, the former may be called *verbal* Predicables. Real Predicables belong to Metaphysics, verbal to Logic.

The case of PROPERTY is different. A Property supposes something not contained in the definition of the name; though it constantly accompanies the thing signified. That any two sides of a triangle are together greater than the third side, is always true; but the truth is not comprised in the meaning of the word triangle; nay, three previous Mathematical Propositions are required to prove it. So, when we say that heat causes expansion, we state a Property of heat, certainly not comprehended under the usual meaning of the word.

Thus, as we see, there are Properties of two kinds, one where Uniform Coexistence, another where Uniform Succession, or Causation is announced. The Property of triangles, above mentioned, is a case of the former sort; that of heat, of the latter. Property then, taken in its largest sense, comprehends the relation of Uniform Coexistence, as well as of Uniform Succession.

Lastly, as to Accident. Accidents are divided by Logicians into Inseparable, and Separable. An Inseparable Accident is something which, so far as we have observed, always attends a subject, but which we could conceive to be wanting, without the loss of the characteristics peculiar to the subject, or of any Properties thereto belonging. Thus, we may have never seen, nor heard of, any but white swans; but we can conceive birds similar in all other respects to swans, and having all the properties of the same, except whiteness. There is nothing evidently absurd in the line of the poet,

"Rara avis in terris nigroque simillima cygno,"

as there would be if whiteness were either included in our definition of swans, or supposed to be of necessity inseparable from them.

From this it appears, that an Inseparable Accident is nearly allied to a Property; and in many cases it would probably be difficult to distinguish the two. At all events, the Accident, like a Property, is something *supposed*, at least, to be uniform, whether it be so actually or not, generally some uniform coexistence, as of the colour whiteness, with the other properties of the swan.

A Separable Accident, on the other hand, is not always found, even within the limited range of our experience, not in all the individuals of a species, not even in the same individual at all times. There is a flower called *Lychnis dioica*, or bachelor's button, some specimens of which in the wild state are red, others white, though of the same species. Colour then, here, is a separable accident. "John is at dinner," expresses an accident separable even from the individual, for John is not always at dinner. A separable accident then differs from an inseparable accident as well as from a property, in this, that it is not an invariable but a casual coexistence, or a casual succession of things.

Upon the whole, it appears from this inquiry, that the first three of the scholastic Predicables are merely verbal; while the two latter, if largely understood, comprise a great part of the Predicables which I have proposed. Identity however, and real Existence, find no place in the old classification. Thus, the old classification of Predicables is neither "a purely *formal* generalization," as it has been styled by a very high authority in Logic,[f] nor yet entirely *real*, but partly the one, partly the other. The first three

---

[f] See notes to "Reid's Brief Account of Aristotle's Logic," p. 687 of Reid's works, edited by Sir William Hamilton.

of these Predicables are Logical, Formal, or Verbal; the two latter Metaphysical or Real.

In the Essay concerning Human Understanding,[g] Locke reduces all that can be affirmed or denied about two things, one of another, or, in his language, about two Ideas, to four heads, viz. 1. Identity or Diversity. 2. Relation. 3. Coexistence, or necessary connexion. 4. Real Existence. With respect to the first, Identity, it appears by Locke's own explanation, that he meant not Identity properly so called or absolute sameness, but close resemblance. It is clear also from the context that under Coexistence, or necessary connection, he included invariable succession, or sequence in time; for, as an instance of Coexistence, he brings forward the fact that iron is susceptible of magnetical impressions. And he openly allows that "Identity," in his sense of close resemblance, "and Coexistence, are truly nothing but Relations," of a peculiar kind indeed, and therefore, as he thinks, to be classed apart from Relations in general. Therefore, these Predicables of Locke, though differently classed, comprehend in reality nothing different from mine, and all mine, with one exception, that of absolute identity or sameness, which he has omitted.

Hume, in his first work, "A Treatise of Human

[g] Book IV. Chap. 1.

Nature,"[h] observes that "it may perhaps be esteemed an endless task to enumerate all these qualities, which make objects admit of comparison, and by which the Ideas of *Philosophical* relation are produced. But if we diligently consider them, we shall find that without difficulty they may be comprised under seven general heads, which may be considered as the sources of all *philosophical* relation." He then proceeds to enumerate these seven, which are, 1. Resemblance. 2. Identity. 3. Relations of Space and Time. 4. Relations of Quantity and Number. 5. Degrees of Quality, 6. Contrariety. 7. The Relation of Cause and Effect. Now the first and second of these are contained in my classification, the third and fourth come under the more general head of Relations of Coexistence, while the fifth and seventh are included under Relations of Succession. There remains, then, only the Relation of Contrariety, which is but a striking difference, a difference which always supposes some resemblance. Were there no resemblance there would be no contrast. A dwarf contrasts well with a giant, less with an elephant, and not at all with a mountain. Contrariety then is included under resemblance. It supposes resemblance in some particulars, perhaps in many, the

[h] Book I. Sect. 5.

absence of it in others. But the mere absence of a relation is no new relation.

In truth, resemblance as much supposes difference as difference resemblance. When we say that one thing resembles another, we in fact affirm that they are not one and the same, and if not the same or identical, there must be differences as well as resemblances. The mind of one man resembles that of another; but how many are the differences! The idea which the same man is conscious of at one time may be as like as possible to the idea which he holds at another; but still there must be between them the difference in the time of their appearance.

Upon the whole then, it appears that the Predicables of Hume are fundamentally the same as mine, only differently arranged, with one exception, that of Real Existence, which he has omitted, probably as not agreeable to his sceptical views. Locke mentions Real Existence, which Hume omits, while Hume mentions absolute Identity omitted by Locke.

Lastly, Mr. Mill, in his System of Logic, enumerates Existence, Coexistence, Sequence, Causation, and Resemblance, and observes that one or other of these is asserted or denied in every proposition, without exception.[1] This classification

---

[1] System of Logic, Book I. Chap. 5.

differs from the one proposed above, in two particulars; first, by classing Causation apart from Sequence, under which I have comprehended it; and secondly, by omitting Identity. This last then is the only important difference.

With these remarks I conclude the subject of Proposition and the Predicables.

## REASONING.

God has given to man two grand means for the advancement of knowledge, and the discovery of truth, OBSERVATION, and REASONING. Some truths are learnt by observation alone, as particular facts submitted to the senses; others, by reasoning alone, as the truths of pure Mathematics; others again, and by far the greater number, by observation and reasoning together. All men know what is meant by observation. Suffice it then to remark that observation is of two kinds; the one exercised upon phenomena over which we have no control; the other, upon changes which we ourselves have induced. The former may be called *natural*, the latter *artificial* observation, for it is exercised upon *experiments*.

Though all men know what observation is, but few, comparatively, know *how to observe* to the best advantage. For observation simply is of very limited use: it may certainly prevent us from falling into a pit, or sinking in a quagmire before our eyes; but unless some inference be drawn from it, no general truth, no science can be established. Consequently, observation is useful, chiefly as a ground for inference, or reasoning; and in common discourse, as well as in many popular works, they are so blended, that it does not readily appear where the one ends and the other begins. Facts, and inferences from facts, are continually confounded by inaccurate speakers and writers.

The nature of Reasoning, and its different kinds are not so generally understood. Though, as we shall afterwards find, there are different sorts of reasoning, yet there must be something common to all, or the name *reasoning* would never have been given to the process in all cases. Our first question then is, what is common to all reasoning?

I. All reasoning is concerned with tracing the *relations* of things, and *inferring* a certain relation of two things from a relation of two or more other things. Such, in Metaphysical language, is the business of Reasoning. In Logical language the same is expressed otherwise, and from one or more *propositions* we are said to *infer* another. What, then, is common to all reasoning, is, that belief in one or more relations, or, when expressed in words, in one or more propositions, leads us on immediately to the belief of another relation, or another proposition, as a cause leads on to its effect.

In all Reasoning, then, some relation or relations, or, when stated in words, some proposition or propositions are granted, and these are called the PREMISES, from which another relation, or another proposition is inferred, that is called the CONCLUSION.

Thus, in order to understand thoroughly the nature of Reasoning, we must know what is meant by a *relation*, and a *proposition*. But these terms have already been explained in full.[k] Suffice it here to repeat, that a relation differs from a perception, or a conception, in this, that it necessarily supposes two things, between which a relation is felt; that the relation, as felt, is a state of mind quite distinct from the conceptions out of which it arises, and that as conceptions are various, so are relations.

These last may all, however, be classed under three heads:

I. Relations of Coexistence;
II. Relations of Succession;

according as they do not, or do, involve the notion of time; and

---

[k] See these words in Philosophical Vocabulary, Part I.

III. Relations of Resemblance, which may, or may not, involve the notion of time.

The Relations of Coexistence are various, such as

1. Relations of Position.
2. Relations of Comprehension, or of a whole to its parts.
3. Relations of Quantity, or more, equal, less, which may be called *exact* Relations, in contradistinction to
4. Relations of Indeterminate Degree.

Relations of Succession, on the other hand, are either of Invariable Succession, or of Casual Succession.

These distinctions will be useful to us in determining the different kinds of Reasoning; but, in the mean time, they are sufficient to show how vast is the field which it embraces.

II. Among the relations now enumerated, those of Quantity deserve peculiar attention, as they alone are *exact* relations, whereby they are clearly distinguished from all others. And as the relations are exact, so likewise is the reasoning built upon them. All reasoning, therefore, may be divided into two sorts; the Demonstrative, or strictly *a priori* Reasoning, and the Probable, or strictly *a posteriori* Reasoning; the one independent of experience, the other dependent thereon, either immediately or remotely. Demonstrative

Reasoning is confined to Mathematics, or the science of Quantity, and contrary to what is often thought, is not founded on general principles or axioms, but on self-evident particular truths. The evidence of the propositions of Euclid does not rest upon the axioms placed at the beginning of the work, but upon the particular instances of those axioms which occur in any proposition. Thus, when in the first proposition we show that, in the triangle

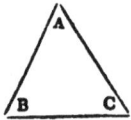

A B C, the side A B is equal to the side B C, and the side A C to B C, we conclude at once, without the intervention of any general axiom, that the side A B is equal to the side A C. The general axiom, that things which are equal to the same are equal to one another, cannot make the conclusion one whit more evident than it was before. We see at once from the particular *data* that such must be the conclusion, or if we do not, no general axiom can convince us. The truth then of the Propositions of Euclid does not rest upon the axioms, nor were they first demonstrated from these. The axioms are placed there *pro forma*, and give a more scientific air to the whole, but they are not necessary.

As particulars must be known before we can generalize, so particular instances of the truth, that "things which are equal to the same are equal to one another," must have been noticed, before we could state it in the form of an universal axiom. Not that the axiom is proved by an induction of particulars, as some affirm, but only that particulars were necessary to allow us to conceive the general proposition. As soon as conceived, its truth is self-evident. Still less, (if in such a matter *degree* were possible) is the general proposition required to prove the particular instances. In like manner, having proved any proposition of Euclid, in a particular case, the mind instantly generalizes the truth; for it sees that what has been proved in the instance before it, must hold good in all other instances where the *data* are exactly similar.

All the Reasonings of pure Mathematics are Demonstrative, and the conclusions arrived at are alone certain and eternal; for first, they start from self-evident or necessary truths, and the mind sees that they are, and always must be so; secondly, the names employed are names of universals, which exist not as real matters of fact; thirdly, these universals belong to Quantity alone, and so admit of an exact definition, or, in other words, they can be accurately distinguished one from another; and lastly, the deductions from these self-evident truths and these definitions are seen at each step to be also irresistible, and unchangeable even by Omnipotence.

Since each step in the deduction is self-evident, as well as the first position, the conclusion must be true.

Why do the relations of Quantity, or of Equality and Inequality, alone admit of demonstration? Because the modes or modifications of Quantity alone can be accurately distinguished. One is as distinct from two as from two thousand. This is the case with no other modes. Other modes admit of *indefinite graduation;* not so those of Quantity. These do not *shade* off one into another. It is on account of this *indefinite graduation* that other relations are not susceptible of demonstration.[1]

Taking the above as a specimen of Demonstrative Reasoning in general, and it may be so taken without any danger of error, we see that two previous propositions are necessary to establish any Mathematical conclusion. First we have A B equal to B C, then A C equal to B C, and lastly A B equal to A C. B C may be called the middle term or medium of comparison between A B and A C.

The range of certainty is very limited, com-

---

[1] See Article QUANTITY, in First Part, Philosophical Vocabulary.

prising only the pure Mathematics; for even Mechanical Philosophy, which uses Demonstrative Reasoning, is based upon experience, and therefore it may err; though granting certain principles, such as the Laws of Motion, the deductions from these are infallibly true. That is to say, they are infallibly true, granting these principles, and supposing that *no others* come into play; for it often happens that the conclusions of the Mechanical Philosopher are wrong in reality, because there are in nature other principles which he has not taken into account. Even the pure Mathematician sometimes arrives at absurd conclusions, absurd in material nature, though true in the world of universals, for they follow irresistibly from his *data*, i. e. from self-evident truths, and from his own definitions, which correspond not with things really existing. Such a conclusion is that of the *Asymptote*, or a straight line, which, though continually approaching, can never meet a certain curve.[m]

[m] If even perfect Ratiocination, such as the Mathematical, may lead to conclusions absurd in material nature, surely the best possible Ratiocination on other subjects may also lead to absurdities. Some German Philosophers of the present day, men of much thought, have *reasoned* themselves into PANTHEISM! It is the business of Experience to correct the errors of pure Reasoning. Bacon has admirably pointed out the dangers of Rationalism as well as of Empiricism. Nov. Org. Lib. I.

III. All Reasonings, other than those already mentioned, lead to probable conclusions only; because they are all ultimately based upon facts known by experience, which is always fallible; for facts may be inaccurately observed, wrong conclusions may be drawn from them, and even what once was fact may cease to be so.

Although all probable reasonings are based ultimately upon facts, real or supposed, yet they do not all arise immediately from the experience of particular things, which alone is properly experience. Some reasonings, no doubt, do so spring, but others start from general principles, or general facts, which had been inferred from many particulars by a previous mental operation. Hence, a well-marked distinction between the INDUCTIVE and the DEDUCTIVE method. The one *brings in* particular facts in order to establish a conclusion, whether general or particular; the other, from some general proposition, deduces or *draws out* a less general proposition. Induction may proceed not only from particulars to particulars, and from particulars to the general, but also from the general to the *more* general; while Deduction always proceeds from a general proposition to one *less* general. The latter is often called *a priori* reasoning, in opposition to the former; though, in reality, the general proposition from which it starts, is known only by induction based upon experience. For instance, when we speculate on the advantages and disadvantages of any form of civil government, we may either consult the history of nations, in order to determine the result of such a scheme in times past, and then conclude that the same would follow now; and here we reason from immediate experience, or inductively; or we may draw our inferences from the acknowledged principles of human nature, and in this case we reason from remote experience or deductively; for the principles of human nature are known to us only by experience.

It is evident that both these methods of inquiry lead not to infallible, but only to probable conclusions. For, besides false accounts of facts, the connection between the premises, namely, a number of particular effects, and the inference that such a thing is the cause of these effects, and of innumerable others similar, is never irresistible; because there is no self-evident absurdity in supposing any thing to be the cause of any thing, and also, because we never can be sure that the cases actually tried, and those not yet tried, are in all respects similar. And though the axioms established by induction be true *generally*, yet, as they seldom are *universally*, as their limits are not defined with perfect accuracy, and as there may be other and counteracting principles at work, therefore, reasoning from these general axioms cannot lead to certain conclusions.

Instance of a general law of nature established by induction.

From the fall, first of an apple, then of other bodies to the earth, Newton inferred, first, that all bodies tend to the earth, and then, that all the bodies in nature tend to each other, the earth, the moon, the planets, the sun, and all that therein is, in a word, that gravitation is universal.

Instances of a general practical maxim obtained by induction.

"For this, Thou shalt not commit adultery, Thou shalt not kill, Thou shalt not steal, Thou shalt not bear false witness, Thou shalt not covet; and if there be any other commandment, it is briefly comprehended in this saying, namely, Thou shalt love thy neighbour as thyself."[a]

The superiority of a standing army over a militia, as to warlike efficiency, is proved *inductively* from the history of many nations, particularly of the ancient world, when standing armies were not universal, and when those who had them conquered the rest; and *deductively* from the general principle of division of labour.

[a] Romans xiii. 9.

There is an antecedent improbability against miracles, founded on our experience of the uniformity of the course of nature; but the truth of a particular miracle, as the raising of Lazarus, may be proved by particular facts in evidence. Here we have first a deduction, then an induction.

The necessity, or, at least, the utility of local government in general, is proved *inductively* from the history of particular nations, some being the seat of government, others ruled as provinces; and the same conclusion is arrived at *deductively* from the known principles of human nature; such as, that persons on the spot better understand, and are more interested in their own affairs, than strangers. Again, the utility of local government in general being proved, the expediency of the same in a particular case, as in that of Ireland, follows by *deduction*; and a like conclusion is established *inductively*, by a reference to the particular history of Ireland.

Take another specimen of deduction. A man is accused of a certain crime, say of murdering another. Starting from certain general principles of human nature, or from the previous general character of the individual in question, we argue that it is very improbable that he committed the murder. This is often called *a priori* reasoning, because it draws a conclusion *prior* to an examination of the particular parts of the case; though in reality it is founded on experience, on experience of human nature in general, or of the individual more especially. Afterwards, many particular facts are brought forward to prove that he actually committed the deed; and from these facts we draw our particular conclusion *inductively.*

What is called Analogical Reasoning, is no distinct species, but only a variety of inductive reasoning. It may be called indirect induction. No better specimen of this can be given than the general strain of the Reasoning contained in Butler's Analogy, of which I shall here give one or two instances. It is supposed to be known by experience that even here there is a moral government, that the good, generally speaking, if not more prosperous outwardly, are more happy inwardly than the wicked. Hence the inference that the same will hold good hereafter; in other words, that the future state will be one of rewards and punishments according to desert.

Again, natural religion is attended with great difficulties: hence, it is probable from analogy, that a system of revealed religion shall not be altogether free from them.

Our own existence, particularly the union of

soul and body is a great mystery, and even seems to involve contradictions; surely then, it is probable that religion shall have mysteries. The soul, from the nature of spirit, can exist in no place: but we believe that it is united to our body, which does exist in space; that where our body is, there also is our soul, and nowhere else. Is the mystery of the Trinity more incomprehensible than this?

Since analogy signifies likeness or resemblance, and analogical reasoning is reasoning from like things to like; wherein, it may be asked, lies the difference between this and other varieties of inductive reasoning? For all induction is from similar to similar; whether from similar causes we infer similar effects, and *vice versa;* or whether from likeness in some part of the chain we infer likeness in the whole chain, without knowledge of causes; as when, from certain appearances of the sky, we predict, perhaps long beforehand, the coming weather; or whether from certain parts we infer the coexistence of other parts, as the experienced anatomist, who, from a single bone, or even fragment of a bone, can construct the whole animal. Inductive reasoning is a species, of which analogy is a variety; nor can we lay down any very definite distinction between it and other varieties. Only, when along with the similarity there is also a good deal of difference, there we call the reasoning analogical; as when we reason from the order of things in this life to that in a future state. Perhaps, the argument by which we establish the existence of the great Creator may be classed under the same head; for the instances of design in the universe, though palpable and innumerable, differ in many respects from those which we find in the works of man. But the similarity is sufficient to render the argument quite convincing; while the differences prove only the immeasurable superiority of the great First Cause.[o]

As a specimen of a chain of Deductive Reasoning, take the following:—

The capacity of the mind is limited;

*Therefore*, the more it is occupied with one thing, the less can it be occupied with another;

*Therefore*, the more it is taken up with intellectual pursuits, the less can it be taken up with the affections, and *vice versa*.

*Therefore*, again, the more it is occupied with general benevolence, the less can it be occupied

---

[o] For an admirable specimen of Analogical Induction, see the opening chapters of Paley's Natural Theology. Never was argument better put. Man ought to consider it as his greatest privilege, that he can by reason find out God.

with private attachments, and *vice versa*. In this reasoning, each proposition is less general than the preceding, and each is an inference from what went before.

From the above examples and observations, the distinction between the inductive and the deductive method of inquiry seems to be clearly established. But when we come to examine the matter more narrowly, we shall perhaps find that there is not so much difference between the *reasonings* employed in these two cases, as we might at first suppose.

Let us remark that the term Induction comprehends two distinct mental operations; first, the observing, the comparing, the selecting of facts; and secondly, an inference drawn from them. The first part of this process is peculiar to induction; for deduction collects not particular facts, it states a general proposition; but both agree in drawing an inference from premises. Now the question is, whether this inference be or be not drawn upon the same principle in both cases?

In Deductive Reasoning, having stated a general proposition, our object is to show that the particular case which we have in view is really comprehended under the general rule; so that if the one be true, so must the other. Thus, our general proposition being, that "the more the mind is occupied with one thing, the less can it be occupied with another," we then consider that intellectual pursuits are an occupation; and again, that the affections are another occupation; whence it appears that the less general proposition "the more the mind is occupied with intellectual pursuits, the less can it be occupied with the affections," is a case of the general rule, or comprehended under it.

Now, how stands the case with Inductive Reasoning? Suppose a traveller in a new country to meet with a troop of animals hitherto quite unknown to him; that he catches one, kills and dissects it with the skill of a practised anatomist. One specimen contents him, for he confidently believes that all the rest, so like outwardly, are also alike inwardly. Now, what reason has he for this belief? The mental process necessary to justify his conclusion seems to be as follows.

Here is an animal of a certain make. There are many other animals, to all outward appearances exceedingly like to this and to each other. But, *nature is uniform in her operations, and never deceives us by uniting great differences with such striking resemblances; therefore*, all these animals are alike within as well as without.

Here it is evident that a general proposition is assumed, tacitly or openly; and from this the conclusion is drawn.

Now this is the case in every instance of Inductive Reasoning. Some general principle is always taken for granted, and with this the particular facts are compared before the conclusion is drawn. The general principle assumed is commonly, " that nature is uniform in her operations;" or, where human testimony is relied on, " that men will tell the truth where they have no interest to the contrary." Thus, in examining the evidences of Christianity, we are careful to observe whether the first witnesses could have had any motive to spread a false story; and when we have determined that they had none, we infer from the above general principle that they actually spoke the truth. Unless that general principle be sound, there is no *reason* why they should have given a true rather than a false account; just as there is no reason why we should believe one quadruped to be organized inwardly like another quadruped, unless nature be in general uniform in her works and operations.

If the above statement be correct, it follows that induction, when taken to comprise not only the examination of facts, but also an inference from them, always embraces a deductive process of reasoning.

Wherein then, it may be asked, consists the difference between Induction and Deduction proper? The difference is,

*First*, that the facts from which induction springs are never more general than the conclusion;

*Secondly*, that the conclusion always *seems* to follow at once from the facts; for

*Thirdly*, the general propositions, being always the same, and universally acknowledged, are never stated; and

*Fourthly*, there is no such thing as a long chain of inductive reasoning, as there may be of deduction proper, where one inference may follow upon another till we get far away from the original premises; whereas, on the other hand,

*Fifthly*, in induction, the detail of facts may fill volumes. There is, in short, in induction, far less reasoning than in deduction proper, the process consisting in the former of one step only.[p]

*Lastly*, since particulars occur first to the mind, it follows that the inductive must precede

---

[p] Take, as an instance of the one, Malthus on Population, who fills three volumes with facts in support of his principle; of the other, the writings of Ricardo and James Mill on Political Economy.

the deductive process. The general notions and general propositions, from which the latter sets out, must have been established by a previous process of inductive generalization, well or ill performed. Thus, in the order of time, induction comes before deduction.

By many, Bacon has been called the *inventor* of the inductive method, a method, however, as old as the creation, which that eminent genius only brought more into notice, restored, improved, and illustrated.

The general principle which runs through deductive reasoning, and of which every such argument is only a particular application, is, that what is allowed to be true *in general* will be true in a particular case. Thus, suppose it granted that trade ought to be free, we may infer that the corn trade ought to be free. But some one may object that here there is a reason for an exception, that the rule is not applicable to this case. Hereupon issue is joined, and the discussion turns upon the point, not whether trade in general ought to be free, for that is granted, but whether there be any circumstances peculiar to the corn trade, which take it out of the general rule; and according to the solution of this question, the above inference will, or will not, hold good.

Now, as we have seen that every case of induction comprises a process of deductive reasoning, it follows that the general principle just mentioned must be common to both deduction and induction. But, besides this common principle, every purely deductive argument has its own less general principle, such as in the above instance, " trade ought to be free," from which a special conclusion is drawn.

In induction, on the other hand, each argument has not a principle peculiar to itself; it has only one or other of two or three very general principles, common to all cases of induction, such as " nature is uniform in her works and operations." Thus we rise from the particular to the general by a process, which, comparing the expressed premises with the conclusion, is the reverse of the deductive; though, as we have seen, the inference from the particular facts to the general law cannot be logically drawn without the intervention of a much more general but universally acknowledged principle.

The object of general induction is to establish a general conclusion, by means of instances so divested of peculiar circumstances as to obviate the mistake of stating as general what is only particular. One instance would be as good as a thousand, if we could be sure that it was quite in point, that is, free from any peculiar circumstances, and it is only because we are not sure of this, that we must multiply instances. The grand point then is to prove similarity, perfect, or at least sufficient similarity, between cases observed and others not observed. The uncertainty of induction depends partly on the difficulty of determining the degree of similarity between cases observed and others which have not been observed in all points, partly on the mistakes to which the original observation was liable. In a word, we may observe ill in the first instance, or the new cases may not be in all respects similar to the old.

There is a strong tendency in the human mind to draw a general conclusion, even from a single instance. Thus, when a child first sees a pool of water, he can form no idea of the effects of water on man; but let him once see a person drowned, and he will ever afterwards act on the belief that water will drown those who get over head and ears. Here the child reasons inductively, and from a single instance, and yet, in this case, correctly. This, and innumerable similar cases, show us the natural tendency, which is to leap at once to a general conclusion, even from one fact observed, a tendency which a wider experience alone can check, and which, in many, if not in all, is checked but imperfectly during the whole course of their lives.

We have seen that the validity of Inductive Reasoning rests fundamentally upon the tacit assumption, that nature is uniform in her operations; that things which have coexisted will be found again to coexist, and that those which have succeeded each other will continue to succeed in the same order. Now, this assumption is not self-evident, neither does it admit of proof; but we implicitly believe, and cannot help believing it to be true. It is then one of the first principles of human knowledge, though not a necessary or self-evident proposition. That the sun which has risen every day of our lives will again rise to-morrow, that when it shines it will give sensible heat, that a stone thrown up into the air will speedily fall back to the earth, we cannot doubt, though the only ground for this belief is, that such has always been the case in time past. Between the assertion, this has always been, and the inference, this will always be, there is a wide gulf, which we must leap across, for we never can bridge it over. The inference is not logical, for we can see no connection between the premises and the conclusion, but it is irresistible. This, then, is a primary article of belief, totally independent of reasoning; neither self-evident, nor known by experience; for experience is only of the past. All inferences from experience, however, take it for granted; and on this assumption alone are they logically drawn.

As the subject of induction has lately given rise to a controversy between two eminent philosophers, I shall conclude what I have to say under this head by a reference thereto; and by examining the points in dispute, I may perhaps be able to throw some additional light upon this fundamental question. The points in dispute between Dr. Whewell and Mr. Mill, so far as the *nature* of induction is concerned, seem to be the following.[q]

1. Whether the term *induction* may with propriety be applied to the case where particular facts are brought in to establish not a general, but a particular conclusion.

2. Whether general facts of every day notoriety, learnt without effort, and commonly called practical knowledge, such as the freezing of water by cold, and its evaporation by heat; the fact that water will suffocate, and fire consume; and the like, be known by a process similar to that whereby truths less familiar, commonly called scientific, are established.

[q] See Dr. Whewell's little work "Of Induction," and Mr. Mill's "System of Logic."

3. Whether the skill which is gained by practice, without formal study, skill in playing cricket, tennis, billiards, &c., skill in shooting with the gun or the bow, &c., when not derived from scientific principles of which the mind is conscious, be, or be not, acquired by a process similar to induction, so similar as to warrant us in applying to it the same name.

Now, in order to solve these questions, we must call to mind what was stated at the opening of this inquiry into reasoning, viz. that God has given to men but two means for the acquisition of knowledge, and the discovery of truth,—observation (including experiments,) and reasoning. Therefore, all knowledge must be acquired either by observation alone, or by reasoning alone, or by the two combined.

Particular facts cognizable by the senses are known simply by observation; as the geographical features of any country, the form of the coast, the course of the rivers, the position of the mountains. That Cambridgeshire is a flat country, Wales mountainous, and Westmoreland abounding in lakes, are facts known by observation alone, at least in the first instance. Here no reasoning is required. On the contrary, the truths of pure Mathematics are known by reasoning alone; for, except the definitions, axioms, and postulates, the first of which are, of course, propositions merely explaining the meaning of words; the second, truths self-evident; the third, self-evident possibilities; the whole process is reasoning.

All other truths, whether general or particular, are acquired by observation, together with reasoning; either by the close union of the two, or by reasoning, based indeed upon observation, following it for a season, but afterwards emancipated from it. To the former of these we conceive that the term *induction* properly belongs. At least, as the process is similar, whenever observation and reasoning closely unite, there the same name should be applied, whether Induction or any other.

In the case of Induction, (upon which Probable Deduction is always founded) the reasoning is based not on necessary or self-evident truths, but on what may be called primary, universal articles of belief, articles neither self-evident, nor capable of proof, which nevertheless we hold with unshaken constancy; such as, belief in the existence of the material world, belief in the uniformity of nature, &c. Starting from these fundamental articles, and taking observation as our guide, we arrive at the knowledge of *general* truths, not cognizable by the senses, by a process combining reasoning with observation, to which the name Induction is always applied. Now, the question is, whether, by a process exactly similar, we may not obtain the knowledge of *particular* facts also, not cognizable by the senses of the inquirer.

Let the particular fact to be established be the genuineness of the Gospel according to St. John. This is a fact certainly not cognizable by the senses of any one now alive, and which cannot therefore be known by observation alone. Neither can it be known by reasoning alone. Therefore, if it can be established, it must be by observation and reasoning together. The particular kind of evidence to which we here have recourse is that of testimony, the testimony of many ancient authors, who cite that Gospel as the undoubted production of St. John. Here we have a number of particular facts, brought forward to establish another particular fact, the principle being always assumed, (though tacitly,) that, generally speaking, human testimony is worthy of credit. Thus, we arrive at the conclusion, that the Gospel attributed to St. John was really written by him. Now, in what does this differ from any case of Induction where the conclusion is general ? Simply in that, not in the process whereby the conclusion is established. We select a great number of particular facts, in this case particular testimonies, all tending to the same conclusion; we then assume, tacitly indeed, the general principle founded on observation, that men will speak truth when they have no decided motive to the contrary; and lastly, we infer that the Gospel of St. John is a genuine work.

The whole process consists, first, in the selection and bringing forward of particular facts; secondly, in the assumption of a general principle universally acknowledged, and therefore seldom openly stated; lastly, in drawing the inference from these premises. We may if we please establish a specific difference, and call this a case of Particular Induction, but we cannot allow that there is a generic distinction between it and General Induction.

In Paley's Evidences of the Truth of Christianity, we find distinct specimens of both Inductive and Deductive inquiry. In chapter i. the author produces evidences of the sufferings of the first propagators of christianity, from the *nature of the case*, that is, he endeavours to show from the known principles of human nature, that persons situated as were undoubtedly the first propagators of christianity, were *likely* to endure much persecution. Here he proceeds Deductively. He afterwards brings forward the testimony of both heathen and christian writers in proof of the same; and here he adopts the Inductive method; as also in the great chapter ix. divided into eleven sections, wherein he enumerates so many direct testimonies in favour of the genuineness of the Books of the New Testament. These we conceive are specimens of Particular Induction, for the facts established are of that order.

To take another and familar instance. Suppose a man, previously in good health, to change his residence. Not long after, he feels indisposed, and he begins to think that the air of his new abode is unwholesome. This is a mere suspicion, for many other causes may have injured his health. However, he leaves his new house, and soon after his usual good health returns. His suspicion is now strengthened; but he is not yet certain. He returns, and again falls ill; now, he has but little doubt. Again he leaves, and again he recovers; at last he is convinced. If the experiment were tried upon other persons, and always with like results, one must be almost as sure of the unhealthiness of the spot, as of a proposition in Geometry. The conclusion in this case is particular, and if it have not been arrived at by induction, I should like to know what name must be given to the process.

The second question is, whether general facts of every day notoriety, learnt without effort, such as the freezing of water by cold, and its evaporation by heat, the fact that water will suffocate, and fire consume, and other such, be known by a process similar to that whereby facts less familiar, commonly called scientific, are established? Dr. Whewell seems to think that the term Induction should be applied only to the process whereby scientific facts are discovered. But we must remember that there is no accurate distinction between scientific and other general facts, no difference except in the degree in which they happen to be familiar. Thus what is considered a vulgar ordinary fact in one country, or in one age, may be science in another place, or at another time. The freezing of water at a certain temperature is a common occurrence in England, but to a native of the coast of Guinea it may be a scientific fact. But will it be said that the knowledge of a familiar fact is obtained in a different manner from a non-familiar one? The only difference, as I conceive, is in the degree of effort, and in the degree of attention required in the two cases. The one we cannot help knowing if we have our eyes open, and enjoy a common share of intellectual faculties; the other may require long and painful investigation.

Still the nature of the process may be essentially the same. The degree of attention and of effort are variable accidents, not essentials, and in no two cases may they quite agree. But what we conceive to be alike in all these cases, is, that we begin by observation, whether with a previous intention or not, and from this observation, combined with a general article of belief, either original or derived, we draw a conclusion less general, which we afterwards apply in particular instances.

Thus, to recur to an example formerly given, there can be little doubt that, were a child of a certain age, with his faculties well developed, to see a man drowned, he would avoid deep water ever afterwards. But why should he avoid it? Surely because he thinks that it would drown him too. And why does he think so? Because he has seen a man drowned. But that alone is no reason. He must conclude from that particular event that water will drown all men, and therefore himself, before he can be said to believe or act rationally. And how can he draw such a conclusion but by means of an original principle of belief, that what has been, will be, or that nature is uniform in her operations? And here we have an exact specimen of the inductive process. Observe well, that this is not instinct, for instinct acts prior to experience, and uniformly, as bees, who, all over the world, build their cells in the form of hexagons; and as some animals, who avoid poisonous plants without trying them. But the child, before experience, does not know that water will suffocate, or fire give pain; for children who have learnt no better will put their fingers into the candle.

Neither can we allow, with Dr. Whewell, that the mere badness or insufficiency of the investigation, or that the falsity of the conclusion, is a sufficient reason for denying that the process is inductive. We constantly say, that a man reasons ill, that his conclusions are erroneous; but we do not for that contend that he does not reason at all. So, a man may content himself with a very wretched induction, and yet he may use it after a fashion of his own. Even the Kentish clown, who said that Tenterden Church Steeple was the cause of the Goodwin Sands, because it was built just before the sea rose and swallowed up the land, may be said to have reasoned inductively. If we adopt the maxim *post hoc*, ergo *propter hoc*, we may prove any absurdity.

I am glad to find that the opinion here stated is held by a distinguished Metaphysician, Dr. Reid:—"The last kind of probable evidence I shall mention, is that by which the known laws of nature have been discovered, and the effects which have been produced by them in former ages, or which may be expected in time to come. The knowledge of some of the laws of nature is necessary to all men in the conduct of life. These are soon discovered even by savages. They know that fire burns, that water drowns, that bodies gravitate towards the earth. They know that day and night, summer and winter, regularly succeed each other. As far back as their experience and observation reach, they know that these have happened regularly, and upon this ground, they are led, by the constitution of human nature, to expect that they will happen in time to come, in like circumstances.

The knowledge which the philosopher attains of the laws of nature differs from that of the vulgar, not in the first principles on which it is grounded, but in its extent and accuracy. He collects with care the phenomena that lead to the same conclusion, and compares them with those that seem to contradict or to limit it. And what conclusions does the philosopher draw from the facts he has collected? They are, that like events have happened in former times in like circumstances, and will happen in time to come; and these conclusions are built on the very same ground on which the simple rustic concludes that the sun will rise to-morrow."

But the dignity of science is thought to be lowered by applying a scientific term to a process in use among the vulgar; and hence, we may suppose, the unwillingness of some peculiarly distinguished in the paths of science, to allow that common knowledge is really acquired by Induction.

The third question is, whether the skill which is gained by practice, without formal study, skill in playing cricket, tennis, billiards, &c., skill in shooting with the gun or the bow, &c., when not derived from scientific principles of which the mind is conscious, and which it can state in words, be or be not acquired by a process similar to Induction, so similar as to warrant us in applying to it the same name.

It is supposed then, that the skill is *acquired*, not *instinctive*, and therefore, so far, it agrees with knowledge the result of Induction. And how is it acquired? By practice, as the phrase is; that is, by experience; not by simple observation, but by numerous intentional trials or experiments. So far, again, it agrees with inductive speculative knowledge. And the performer is supposed to improve by experience. But how

* Reid on the Intellectual Powers, Essay vii.

can he improve unless he have paid attention to the circumstances attending his successes, and his failures, and have thence drawn some general conclusions, some rules applicable to future occasions? What though these rules be not formally stated in propositions? What though they cannot be imparted to others? They may, notwithstanding, exist in his mind in a shape sufficiently definite to act upon, and indeed we may be sure that they do so exist, otherwise no practice would make him better.

Very similar is the case of what is commonly called practical knowledge in a learned profession, as in that of the Physician. All the study in the world will never make a good physician without experience of the treatment of diseases; and some gain more from the same experience than others. The same *outward* facts are before all, but some learn much from them, others little, that is to say, they make more or fewer, better or worse inductions. Much of this knowledge is incommunicable, and so dies with the individual, because it is not sufficiently definite, subject to too many exceptions, to be formally stated in propositions. So it is with games of skill, such as cricket, or tennis. Some rules of good play may certainly be stated in words, but others cannot for the reason just given. But, because they cannot be enunciated, we must not conclude that they exist not mentally; and that they do exist, the best proof is that progress is made.

How can progress be made in any thing, speculative or practical, without an operation of mind? To move our limbs requires a previous mental change, and though muscular strength must exist, it is the mind that directs. To suppose that the mere muscular fibre can *prefer* one action to another, is as contradictory as to affirm that body is mind, that matter is spirit. Skill in bodily motion, then, always supposes a previous mental training; but there can be no mental training without rules, and no rules without induction.

On each of the three questions above stated, I am thus led to a conclusion the reverse of that at which Dr. Whewell has arrived. On other points, however, I am glad to find that I agree with that eminent philosopher. It is debated between him and Mr. Mill, whether Kepler's discovery of the law, that the planets move round the sun in ellipses, be, or be not, an instance of Induction. That it is, I completely agree with Dr. Whewell. Why is the contrary maintained by Mr. Mill? "Because," says he, "it is a fact, surely, that the planet does describe an ellipse, and a fact which we could see, if we had adequate visual organs, and a suitable position."[*]

The whole pith of this objection lies in the Conjunction *if*.

It is quite true that if we had such organs, and such a position, we should have no need of induction to establish the fact in question; we should require our senses only, and the faculty of perception. We require no induction to prove that the Pantheon at Rome is round, and the Colosseum oval. But these we can take in with a glance; and it is exactly because we cannot so embrace the orbits of the planets, that Induction is necessary to establish the fact of their ellipticity. What Kepler really saw was a planet in many different positions, and nothing more; he could not see it moving, still less could he see its whole course at once. How then could he possibly *describe* its orbit, as Mr. Mill supposes? for we describe only what we see. From many different positions then, which he actually saw, he *inferred* innumerable other positions which he did not see, all which together made up this figure of an ellipse. I cannot conceive a fairer specimen of Induction; though in this case, no law of causation was established. But the discovery of causes, though the highest

[*] System of Logic, Ratiocinative, and Inductive, Vol. I. p. p. 363.

end of Induction, is not essential to the process.

Can it be that Mr. Mill will allow this to be only a *description*, because the elliptical form of the orbit is a *fact*? But as I have shown under the article "Hypothesis and Theory," and as Dr. Whewell also maintains, a fact differs from a theory only in the degree of evidence on which it rests. A theory well established, and generally received, becomes a fact. This is a truth without the knowledge of which, there can, as I conceive, be no correct estimate of the object of science and philosophy.

I also entirely agree with Dr. Whewell, that a conception is an essential part of induction. Indeed, I am at a loss to imagine how the contrary can be maintained by any metaphysician. If we do not *conceive* a general fact before enunciating it in words, we must then, I suppose, *perceive* it. We may certainly perceive particular facts, such as the fall of a stone to the earth, but how can we perceive that all bodies within a certain distance would fall to the earth, or that all bodies in nature tend to each other? These are general facts far removed from our senses, and therefore from our perceptions, which are closely connected with our sensations. A simple *tendency* cannot be seen even in a particular instance, still less a general tendency. But the mind conceives it, otherwise how could we know it? If it be allowed that we know anything, and yet we do not perceive it, I should like to know what word we ought to employ better than conception to express that knowledge?

Unless we revive the exploded and unphilosophical notion of Condillac, that all our mental states are only *transformed sensations;* unless we allow with Destutt de Tracy, that "Penser c'est sentir et rien que sentir," we cannot get rid of conceptions, in cases where we know, suppose, conjecture, or imagine, but do not perceive.

It is allowed that Kepler did not see, did not perceive the elliptical orbit of the planets, or of any one planet. Yet he affirmed, with more or less certainty, that the orbit was such. But how could he affirm that of which he had no notion or conception? The supposition is a palpable contradiction.

I likewise think with Dr. Whewell, that Mr. Mill has made a great mistake in supposing that the future progress of science will depend more upon deduction than induction. Nothing appears to me more unlikely. If we compare the slow progress of physical science before the triumph of the inductive method under Bacon, with its rapid progress since, we shall be convinced that its future advancement must still depend upon the same method. Every year, almost every month, some new discovery is announced as thus obtained, and who shall say when these discoveries shall be exhausted? If we consider that it is little more than two hundred years since men began seriously and patiently to investigate nature, we shall rather conclude that inductive science is, as yet, in its infancy. In the history of the human race, two hundred years is but a point.

To many of the physical sciences deduction is applicable in a very limited degree, and no reason at present appears why it should ever be much more applicable. It enters little into the sciences of Chemistry, Physiology, Geology, or Meteorology; still less into the purely descriptive sciences of Zoology, Botany, and Mineralogy.

Before the triumph of the Baconian Philosophy, physicians attempted to account for all the phenomena of life from a few principles of Chemistry or of Mechanics; with what success all are now agreed.

It is chiefly in the Mental Sciences, and in Mechanical Philosophy, which treats of sensible motions, that deduction plays an important part. In morals, and politics, innumerable volumes have been filled in deducing conclusions from a few general principles. The whole philosophy of Bentham is a deduction from his one principle of self-interest.

So it is likewise in Mechanical Philosophy; where, from a few general facts established by experience, such as the laws of motion, we are able to deduce innumerable conclusions by reasoning strictly demonstrative. The sensible motions of inanimate matter, and the actions of rational voluntary agents, seem then to afford the greatest scope for deductive inquiry. Insensible motions, on the other hand, such as those of Chemistry, and even the sensible motions of living bodies, cannot be traced far in this way.

It would, however, be a fatal mistake to suppose, that little or nothing remains to be done in the mental sciences by means of induction. Pure Mental Philosophy or Metaphysics, is more of an inductive than of a deductive science. It is by observing the operations of our own minds that we come to know them, and it is exactly because that observation was so neglected, that Metaphysics made so little progress.[*] And who shall pretend to say, that all the social and political lessons of history are exhausted, that no

---

[*] For an example of the application of the inductive method to mental philosophy, see the Author's "Analysis and Theory of the Emotions."

new principles remain to be discovered, that we have only to apply the old? It is not many years since Malthus established the principle of population by a very copious induction. It seems to me the more remarkable that Mr. Mill should have undervalued the probable efficacy of induction in the future progress of science, seeing that so large a part of his own great work is devoted to the subject. I cannot but consider this as the most important part of his system of Logic. His attempt to reduce induction to a scientific form appears to me worthy of all commendation. Dr. Whewell, I am aware, thinks otherwise, and he is fortified by the opinion of Sir John Herschel, as well as by another eminent author, who look upon the corresponding efforts of Bacon, the "prerogatives of instances," contained in the second book of the Novum Organum, as more curious than useful. But the objections made to such attempts are nothing new; they are the same as have been started against Logic in general, as well as against scientific systems of morals, viz., that men use induction naturally, reason naturally, praise and blame naturally, and therefore there is no occasion for science in these matters. We grant the premises, but deny the conclusion. Men, it is true, use induction naturally, but often imperfectly; they reason naturally, but often inconclusively; they praise and blame naturally, but not always justly. Hence the utility of general rules applicable to induction, to reasoning in general, and to moral sentiment."

I shall conclude this head with one of the Aphorisms of Bacon, wherein the two methods, the Deductive and the Inductive, are well described.

"There are and can be but two ways of seeking and finding out truth. The one, from sense and particulars flies to the most general axioms, and from these principles, firmly established, finds out and judges of intermediate axioms; and this is the way now in use. The other raises axioms from sense and particulars,

---

" The argument in favour of the application of Science to Reasoning, as well as to Morals, may be seen, for the one, in the Introduction to Whately's Elements of Logic; for the other, in the Introduction to my own Principles of Human Happiness and Human Duty. With respect to the utility of the rules of the Novum Organum in particular, the opinion of Dr. Reid differs widely from that of Dr. Whewell and Sir John Herschel. Among those philosophers who have most closely pursued the path pointed out in that great work, he mentions Sir Isaac Newton as holding the first rank; "having in the third book of the *Principia*, and in his *Optics*, had the rules of the *Novum Organum* constantly in his eye." " Brief account of Aristotle's Logic, Chap. vi. Sect. 2.

ascending continuously and gradually, so as at last to arrive at the most general; which is the true but untried way."[x]

Though these two modes of inquiry, Induction, and Deduction, embrace a very large part of probable reasoning, yet there seem to be some reasonings, which cannot properly be classed under either. As instances, take the following:

A is the cause of B; but B is the cause of C:
*Therefore*, A is the remote cause of C.

Application depends upon the will; but intellectual advancement depends much upon application:
*Therefore*, intellectual advancement depends much upon the will.

Romulus founded Rome; but Rome conquered great part of the known world, and rose to an unexampled pitch of power and grandeur;
*Therefore*, Romulus was the original cause of the power and grandeur of Rome.

In these, and similar reasonings, we neither rise from particulars to generals, nor descend from generals to particulars; but we remain as it were, *on a plain*, as in pure Mathematics; and from two previous propositions, likewise as in pure Mathematics, we infer a third: whereas in

[x] Novum Organum, Aph. xix.

deductive reasoning, though there may be three propositions when the argument is stated in full, yet, one is very often suppressed; in inductive reasoning always. This, then, I shall beg leave to call *plain reasoning*. Thus, we find, that probable reasoning embraces at least three kinds; the Inductive, the Deductive, and the Plain; and the last seems to approach nearer to the nature of demonstration, than either of the others. In it, no general principle is tacitly assumed and reasoned from, but all is openly stated; and though the last proposition follows from the two former, it is not comprehended under either of them.

Plain reasoning, then, differs much more from the Deductive and the Inductive, than these two from each other. Therefore, they ought not to be classed on the same line. Indeed we have seen, that though the whole process of Induction differs widely from Deduction, yet, the *reasoning*, strictly so called, contained in both, is very similar. Consequently, we ought to class Inductive and Deductive Reasoning together, as species of a common genus, opposed to which, will be Plain Reasoning.

IV. After these remarks on the nature of reasoning in general, as well as its different kinds, we shall be better able to answer that oft-debated question, what are we to think of the SYLLOGISM? In the whole history of philosophy, there is not a more singular fact than this, that the syllogism is still a matter of dispute.

Since the days of Bacon, however, the empire of Aristotle has gradually been going to decay, and faith in the all-sufficiency of the syllogism has more and more been shaken. Bacon himself, in his *Novum Organum*, frequently decries the syllogism;[y] Pascal depreciates it;[z] and Locke, with some succeeding philosophers, particularly Thomas Brown, scoffs at it altogether. But in our days, an attempt has been made to restore the logic, as well as the religion of the middle ages, and the same university which nursed a Newman, has produced a Whately.[a] The latter

---

[y] See *Novum Organum in Distributione operis*, and Aph. xi, xii. xiii. xiv. and lxiii, where Aristotle is blamed for corrupting Physics by his Dialectics. See also *De Augmentis Scientiarum*, Lib. V. Cap. ii.

[z] See Pascal "De l'esprit Geometrique," and "De l'art de persuader," contained in the last and best edition of the "Pensées de Pascal," by Prosper Faugère, Paris 1844.

[a] It is worthy of remark, that Whately, in the Preface to his "Elements of Logic," acknowledges that the Rev. J. Newman "actually composed a considerable portion of the work, as it now stands, from manuscripts not designed for publication;" and that he is "the original author of several pages."

has written a work, chiefly to prove that the Logic of Aristotle is the only Logic, and syllogism the only reasoning; that, in fact, the syllogism is not a particular *kind* of reasoning, but the *form* to which all sound reasoning may be reduced, by whatever name it be called. Thus, according to the Archbishop and Philosopher, there are no different *sorts* of reasoning, but all are alike, whether certain, or probable, *a priori*, or *a posteriori*, demonstrative, inductive, or deductive; all are exactly similar. That the *reasoning*, strictly so called, contained in induction, is akin to deduction, I am willing to allow, and indeed, have endeavoured to show; but, that mathematical or demonstrative reasoning differs not specifically from either, I can by no means admit. This, Dr. Whately assumes without any attempt at proof. What I have called plain probable reasoning seems to me also to differ materially from the deductive, as well as from the inductive.

No doubt there must be something common to all reasoning, or the same name *reasoning* would not have been given to the process in all cases; but had there been no differences, neither would there have been any specific names, such as *probable, demonstrative, inductive*, &c. What is common to all reasoning, what it is which makes reasoning a *genus*, we have seen in the opening of this article; and that account we must bear in mind during the following discussion. Wherein consist the differences which mark out several species of reasoning, we have also seen; and if these differences be real, especially the grand difference between demonstration and probability, then it follows, contrary to the opinion of Whately, that all reasoning is not specifically the same. Consequently, unless the word syllogism *mean* nothing more than a sound argument in general, stated in full, unless it be merely a generic word, then all sound reasoning, stated explicitly, cannot be syllogistical.

But, in order to know what the word *syllogism* really does mean, we must refer to the definitions which have been given of it, the examples brought forward in illustration, and the general principle said to pervade all syllogisms. When we know what a syllogism really is, then, and not till then, can we determine whether it include all reasoning, or any.

Let us first take Aristotle's own definition of the Syllogism, which is as follows:—"A syllogism is a speech in which certain propositions being stated and granted, some other proposition different from these follows of necessity; and this solely in virtue of the propositions stated."[b] And this definition is thus explained by Alexander, one of Aristotle's commentators. "But, when Aristotle says, *follows of necessity*, this does not mean that the conclusion, as a proposition in itself, should necessarily be true; for this is the case only in syllogisms of necessary matter; but, *that the conclusion, be its matter what it may, actual, contingent, or necessary, must follow of necessity from the premises.*"[c]

Reid's definition of syllogism, as completed by Sir William Hamilton, varies a little from the foregoing, but is perfectly consistent with it. "A syllogism," says he, "is an argument, or reasoning, consisting (always explicably or implicibly) of three propositions, the last of which, called the CONCLUSION, is (necessarily) inferred from the (very statement of the) two preceding, which are called the PREMISES."[d]

According to the above definitions, all pure mathematical or demonstrative reasoning is syllogistical; for here, assuredly, each argument con-

---

[b] Prior Analytics, Book I. Chap i.

[c] See Sir William Hamilton's edition of Reid's works, "A brief account of Aristotle's Logic."—Chap. iv. Sect. 5, Note.

[d] The words in brackets have been supplied by Sir William Hamilton in his edition of Reid's works.

sists of three propositions, and the conclusion follows irresistibly, or of necessity, from the premises.

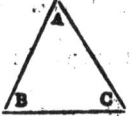

In the triangle A B C, let the side A B be equal to B C, and A C to B C. Then the side A B will be equal to the side A C. Here there are three propositions, the two former being called the premises, from which the conclusion follows irresistibly. And as this is a specimen of all pure mathematical reasoning, therefore, according to the above definition, all such reasoning is syllogistical.

But, in all other reasonings, generally considered sound and valid, does the conclusion follow of necessity from the conclusion?

Take the following as a specimen:—
"Trade (in general) ought to be free,"
Therefore, the corn trade ought to be free.

Is this reasoning, or is it not? Is it good reasoning? Most people, I conceive, would allow that the reasoning is fair, though not infallible. From the assumption that trade ought to be free, we are entitled to infer, *probably* indeed, *not necessarily*, that the corn trade ought to be free; probably only, because, though trade in general ought to be free, there may still be circumstances peculiar to the corn trade which take it out of the general rule. Therefore, here we have a specimen of what all would allow to be reasoning, where the conclusion does not follow of necessity from the premises, and which, therefore, does not agree with the definition of the syllogism. Consequently, all reasoning is not syllogistical in the sense above given.

Moreover, can we say that the argument consists implicitly of three propositions? If there be three, then explicitly they are as follows:—

"Trade (in general) ought to be free."

The corn trade is a trade.

Therefore, the corn trade ought to be free.

Does not every one see that the second proposition is a mere truism, or identical statement, where nothing is told which is not implied in the meaning of the subject of the proposition? It cannot, therefore, be an essential part of the argument; and if not, then we have a valid piece of reasoning, consisting only of two propositions. Here again, then, we miss one of the characteristics of the syllogism. But the above is only a specimen of ten thousand arguments of the same kind; and therefore, we must conclude that all reasoning cannot be stated in syllogisms, as above defined.

Let us now take another method of arriving at the nature of the syllogism, and instead of a definition, let us examine what is allowed by dialecticians to be the fundamental principle of all syllogisms, the famous *dictum* of Aristotle, which is, that *whatever is affirmed or denied universally of any class of things, may be affirmed or denied of anything comprehended in that class.* This, according to Archbishop Whately, is the UNIVERSAL PRINCIPLE of *Reasoning*; for, as he thinks, all reasoning is syllogistical.* Now, can this principle be applied to all reasoning? In the first place, be it remarked, that this celebrated *dictum* is, in reality, no principle or axiom at all, for it affirms nothing which is not already comprehended in the meaning of the word *class*. It is, in fact, a definition of a class, and so a merely verbal proposition. How a mere definition can be the universal principle of reasoning, passes all conception.

But, waving this objection, which meets us at the very outset of the inquiry, and allowing the

---

* Let it not be supposed that I assert that Aristotle thought that he had discovered in this *dictum* the Universal Principle of *Reasoning*. My remarks apply to one of the most distinguished of his modern disciples, and we all know that disciples often go beyond their masters. Aristotle said only that the above *dictum* was the Universal Principle of *Syllogisms*.

above to be entitled to the name of a principle, let us see whether it be applicable to all, or any kind of reasoning. When we refer to the various sorts of relation, about which reasoning is conversant, that are mentioned above, we see but one kind, at most, to which the principle of the syllogism can be applicable, namely, relations of comprehension. This, no doubt, is a very important class, but it is only one class; and certainly not more important than relations of cause and effect. If A be the cause of B, and B of C, then A is the remote cause of C. This is surely reasoning, and correct reasoning; but how the conclusion is here *comprehended* under either of the premises, I am quite at a loss to perceive.

So likewise in the reasoning,

Application depends upon the will:

But intellectual advancement depends much upon application:

Therefore, intellectual advancement depends much upon the will.

Here it will be allowed that the conclusion follows fairly from the premises; but surely, it is not comprehended under either of them. According to the syllogistic theory, application is here the middle term, and this is a class under which the subject of the conclusion, namely, intellectual advancement, must be brought, in order that what had previously been asserted of the former, may be asserted also of the latter. But, how intellectual advancement is a particular instance, or a species, of the genus application, I am at a loss to see. By the supposition, the one, application, precedes as cause, and the other, intellectual advancement, follows as effect; and therefore, the latter cannot be an instance of the former.

Again, taking relations of quantity,

in the triangle A B C, if the side A B is equal to B C, and A C to B C, then is the side A B equal to A C. This, it will be allowed, is demonstrative reasoning; but here also the principle of the syllogism is quite inapplicable. The conclusion certainly follows irresistibly from the premises, but it is not comprehended under either of the previous propositions.

It appears, then, from the acknowledged general principle of the syllogism, and from the particular instances of demonstrative reasoning, and probable plain reasoning, now given, that to neither of these species of reasoning is the syllogism applicable. But we found before, that it follows directly from the definition of the syllogism, that all probable reasoning cannot be stated in syllogisms. Therefore, whether we start from the definition, or from the acknowledged general principle of the syllogism, we arrive at the same conclusion. Mark, however, this difference, that whereas, according to the definition, demonstrative or pure mathematical reasoning is certainly syllogistical; according to the general principle above stated, it certainly is not syllogistical. Therefore, the definition and the general principle are inconsistent; but, whether we adopt the one or the other, it equally follows that all reasoning cannot be expressed in syllogisms.

The question is now reduced to much narrower limits. Having seen that the syllogism is not the form in which *all* correct reasoning can be stated, it only remains to inquire whether *any* legitimate reasoning can be so expressed.

If we take the definitions above given of the syllogism, that question is already answered; for we found that demonstrative or mathematical reasoning agrees perfectly with those definitions. But, as they are in accordance neither with the so-called general principle of the syllogism, nor yet with the examples thereof generally brought forward, we shall adopt these in order to determine whether *any* reasoning be really syllogistical.

Agreeably to that fundamental principle, as

given above, it would appear, that, to relations of comprehension, if to any, the syllogism must apply; for the principle is, that what is true of a class, is true of all individuals comprehended under that class. To deductive reasoning, then, as tracing relations of comprehension, the syllogism may be applicable.

Observe, that, in reference to reasoning, there are two questions to be solved, the one purely metaphysical and speculative, the other logical and practical: the first, what is really the process which goes on in our minds in reasoning? The second, how are we to test the validity of an argument? Each of these questions must be treated separately.

This distinction may be illustrated by reference to Ethics, in which also there are two grand questions; the one, what are the causes present to the mind, which actually regulate our moral sentiments? The other, what are the circumstances which justify us, on mature reflection, for awarding approbation or disapprobation to any action? The former question relates to the origin of our moral sentiments, the latter to the criterion of morality.

The first question is, whether the syllogism be a full statement, founded on a correct Analysis, of the mental process in deductive reasoning.

Having already mentioned the general principle of the syllogism, let us now bring forward some examples.

1. Whatever exhibits marks of design had an intelligent author.
   The world exhibits marks of design:
   *Therefore*, the world had an intelligent author.
2. All tyrants deserve death.
   Cæsar was a tyrant:
   *Therefore*, Cæsar deserved death.
3. Every dispensation of providence is beneficial.
   Afflictions are dispensations of providence:
   *Therefore*, they are beneficial.
4. Every creature possessed of reason and liberty ought to practice justice.
   Man is a creature possessed of reason and liberty:
   *Therefore*, he ought to practise justice.
5. No vicious man is worthy of esteem and reward.
   John is a vicious man:
   *Therefore*, John is not worthy of esteem and reward.
6. No tyrannical government is good.
   The Turkish government is tyrannical:
   *Therefore*, it is not good.

These are instances of regular syllogisms, in the first *Figure*, to which, we are told by Aristotle and his followers, all legitimate syllogisms may be reduced. Here the middle term is the subject of the major, and the predicate of the minor proposition.' We shall also give a specimen of the second and of the third figure.

7. Whatever is bad is not the work of God.

All the natural passions and appetites of men are the work of God:

*Therefore*, they are not bad.

In this instance, the middle term is the predicate both of the major and of the minor proposition, or the syllogism is of the second figure.

The next is from Reid.

8. All Africans are black.

All Africans are men:

*Therefore*, some men are black.

Here the middle term is the subject both of the major and minor, or the syllogism is of the third figure.

These instances may suffice to show us the nature of syllogisms. In all, the conclusion is

---

' The first three are taken from Whately's Logic. The first in particular is his favourite specimen. In the Prior Analytics, Book I. Chap. vii. Aristotle proves that all syllogisms may be reduced not only to the first figure, but to the two universal *moods* of the first figure, either *directly* by conversion, or *indirectly* by *reductio ad absurdum*.

evident, *provided the premises* be *granted*; and in all, the validity consists in the same thing, which, when stated generally, constitutes the *dictum* above mentioned; namely, that whatever is affirmed or denied *universally* of any class of things, may be affirmed or denied of any thing comprehended in that class. In framing the argument, then, the object is to refer the subject of the conclusion to some class, (middle term) of which class something can be affirmed or denied universally. Thus, in the first syllogism, the subject of the conclusion, "the world," is referred to a class of things, "those which exhibit marks of design," of which it can be universally affirmed that "they had an intelligent author." And so with the rest.

Now the question is, do men actually reason thus? That they do not openly or apparently so reason, every one's experience may convince him. Taking each of the six syllogisms in the first figure, to which form the other figures may be reduced, we shall see that in every case the natural or usual way of reasoning would be confined to the second and third propositions, omitting the first. In order to prove that the world had an intelligent author, none but a dialectician would think of beginning by stating, "whatever exhibits marks of design had an intelligent author;" but an ordinary reasoner would say,

The world exhibits marks of design:

*Therefore*, it had an intelligent author. And so in the other cases.

But though, not expressed, is not the first or major proposition understood? Mentally embraced, though not stated in words? There lies all the question.

When we examine these six syllogisms, we find that the major is always an *universal* proposition, and this, in fact, is one of the laws of the first figure, as it is of syllogisms in general that one of the premises must be universal. Unless this be the case, no infallible inference can be drawn. If the major proposition be universal, it *must* embrace the conclusion, for this is only a particular instance of the same. Consequently, by assuming the major, we assume the conclusion; or, in other words, our first proposition takes for granted the very thing to be proved. And this, we are told, is the legitimate, nay, the only legitimate mode of reasoning! Certainly, of all the delusions that ever passed current in the world, this is the greatest; for it is a delusion not peculiar to the vulgar, but shared, even now, by some of the highest names in philosophy. It is engendered between reverence for antiquity and respect for Aristotle and Greek, and in many instances it has proved too strong, not only for common sense, but for high intellectual powers. On that account it is the more important that the delusion should be expelled.

Aristotle shows (Prior Analytics, Book I. Chap. xxiv.) that unless one of the two propositions which compose the premises be universal, there can be no syllogism. "Thus," says he, "if we have to demonstrate that music is a dignified pleasure, if we state only that pleasure is dignified, without saying all pleasure, there is no syllogism." Strange that this acute philosopher should not have put the question to himself, if all pleasure be dignified, what occasion is there for reasoning to prove that the pleasure of music is so? That question once fairly answered, he might have spared himself the immense trouble of writing the Prior Analytics, a mighty monument of useless ingenuity.

Who, I would ask, starting from the major proposition of the syllogism, would think of proving that Cæsar, as a tyrant, deserved death, *because* all tyrants deserve death? *That is the very thing to be proved.* Whether we use the singular or the plural, it makes no difference; for the general term *Tyrant* comprehends as many particulars as the phrase *all Tyrants*. What can be more silly than the statement, a tyrant, any tyrant, deserves death, *because* all tyrants deserve death? But such, and no other, is the proof afforded us in this syllogism. These two propositions are in reality identical; they differ only in form. We conclude that what, instead of proving any thing, begins by taking for granted the very thing to be proved, cannot be the natural mode of reasoning.

Moreover, the above specimens of syllogism, and others, such as are usually found in books of Logic, in all the varieties of figure and mood, do not answer to the definition of syllogism given by Aristotle above, viz. that "a syllogism is a speech in which certain propositions (the premises) being stated and granted, some other proposition (the conclusion) different from these, follows of necessity; and this solely in virtue of the propositions stated." Now, we have seen that the syllogisms constructed according to the rules of figure and mood, and in agreement with the *Dictum* of Aristotle *de omni et nullo*, as it is called, really bring out in the conclusion nothing different from the premises. Therefore, they do not correspond with the above definition, which, as we have shown, agrees with demonstrative or mathematical reasoning only.⁵ That definition is a definition of perfect or demonstrative reasoning, and if we please to call it syllogistic, well and good: but then we must remember that such syllogisms are very different from the syllogisms of the schools, which alone we are now combating. In these last, the connection between the premises and the conclusion is no doubt irresistible, because the latter is assumed in the former; but for that reason it can contain nothing new, nothing different. Not so in real and perfect reasoning, such as that of Geometry, where the conclusion not only follows irresistibly from the premises, from both together, but where it also contains something different from either.

"In what, then, consists this admirable discovery of the syllogism?" asks Barthélemy Saint Hilaire, in the Preface to his Translation of Aristotle's Organon? "In this," answers he, "that Aristotle first established that reasoning was possible on the one condition alone of starting from a principle, to arrive by the aid of a

⁵ What we have called Plain Reasoning approaches more nearly to the Mathematical than any other, and in some cases seems not to fall short of demonstration: though the *matter* about which it is conversant be *contingent*, not *necessary*. Therefore, though the conclusion follows irresistibly from the premises, it may still be false.

middle term at a conclusion resulting necessarily from that principle." According to this statement, there can be none but demonstrative reasoning; *first mistake*. Again, by this, the conclusion in demonstrative reasoning follows necessarily from the principle, as Saint Hilaire calls it, or major proposition; whereas, in mathematical reasoning, it follows not from one of the premises alone, but from both together; *second mistake*. In the simple reasoning, A is equal to B, and B to C; therefore, A is equal to C; the conclusion certainly follows not necessarily from either of the two premises, but from both, and the one is no more entitled to be called a principle than the other. It is only in the fictitious reasoning of the syllogism, that the conclusion follows necessarily from the major proposition, *because in that proposition the conclusion is taken for granted beforehand*. It may be remarked, that Logicians of a certain class are often at war with the Mathematicians. No wonder; for no science so clearly refutes the absurd pretensions of the School Logic as Mathematics.

I am well aware that a very high authority in Logic maintains that we cannot draw the simplest inference in Mathematics without the use of an universal principle; and that even the reasoning A is equal to B, and B to C, therefore A is equal to C, is elliptical. Stated in full, we are told that reasoning would be as follows:—

What are equal to the same, are equal to each other;

A and C are equal to the same (B);

Therefore, A and C are equal to each other.

How is this question to be determined? By an appeal to consciousness, the supreme tribunal in Metaphysics. To consciouness, then, we do appeal, and we maintain that the reasoning A is equal to B, and B to C, therefore, A is equal to C, is not elliptical; that nothing is wanting to the evidence of the conclusion, that the mind sees that conclusion as resulting from the premises at once and irresistibly. Does any one deny this evidence, and ask for more proof? We have no more to offer, for we cannot give a demonstration of a demonstration. As for what is called the full statement, we deny that it is one whit more satisfactory than the other, or that it is the natural mode of reasoning. It is an artificial mode, invented to prop up a theory by reducing mathematical reasoning to the syllogistic form. We cannot of course support our denial by a formal proof, for the first principles of reasoning admit not of proof; but we confidently appeal to the consciousness of every man of common understanding.

We must not confound analysis with generalization. The reasoning, A is equal to B, and B to C, therefore, A is equal to C, seems to admit of no analysis, it is complete in all its parts, all is expressed; but, when we come to compare this with other examples of reasoning, we find that there is a striking similarity between them, which similarity, or point of agreement, may be stated as a general principle, and formalized in words, thus, "things which are equal to the same are equal to one another." This general principle, then, is said to pervade all such specimens of reasoning; that is, each is a particular instance thereof. But we must not therefore suppose that each is proved from the general principle. On the contrary, but for the particular instances, the general proposition would never have been thought of. It comes after the particular proofs, by a process of generalization, forming an axiom convenient for the purpose of communicating knowledge, and satisfactory to the mind of the learner, as showing at a glance all that he is called upon to take for granted in the ensuing demonstration; but it cannot be necessary to a proof which is evident without it, and which actually was established without it; for few will maintain that the geometrical discoverer began by laying down axioms.

One question only now remains. Though the syllogism be not an accurate detailed statement, derived from a correct analysis of the process of reasoning, is it of any use as a *test*, a *criterion* of the validity of an argument? In other words, though false metaphysically, can it serve any purpose logically?

If the syllogism be not an accurate statement of the full mental process in reasoning, there is surely a strong probability, *a priori*, against its logical utility. But let us examine this point separately.

When we consider the specimens given above, or any others that are in due form, we shall find that what the syllogism does, is to point out in the major proposition what must be taken for granted, in order that the inference may be irrefragable, in other words, that the conclusion may follow necessarily from the premises. In order to show this necessary connexion, or want of connexion, the syllogism so states the case, that the conclusion is evidently comprehended, or not comprehended, under the premises. But then, the major premiss, taken for granted, requires proof, quite as much as the conclusion, nay, more, for it comprehends it, and more also; and therefore, though the *inference* be correct, the *conclusion* may be utterly false; and the reason why the inference is irrefragable, is because the conclusion is taken for granted in the premises; and if it be not taken for granted, then the inference is not irrefragable. The syllogism, in fact, shows nothing more than this; that *unless* such a preliminary proposition be true, we cannot be quite sure of the conclusion. But, as we can be quite sure of no matter of fact, at least of no universal fact, the conclusion must, after all, be hypothetical; though we are apt erroneously to suppose that it is certain, because the inference is correct.

The only conceivable use of the syllogism, is to show us what large assumptions must be made, if we would have a semblance of certainty; and consequently, that there is no real certainty, but only probability. "The world exhibits marks of design," (that is which look like design): "therefore, the world had an intelligent author." It is true that this conclusion cannot be quite certain, unless, " whatever exhibits marks of design had an intelligent author." Neither is it perfectly certain, because "Cæsar was a tyrant," " therefore, he deserved death," unless "*all* tyrants deserve death;" but what ought we to infer from this, but that all our reasonings on matters of fact are fallible, and liable to exceptions ; for, in order that the conclusion may follow irresistibly, universal propositions must be assumed to be true, though as such, they may be false? To impress this truth on the mind, seems to me the only possible advantage to be derived from the syllogism; though its effect has been just the contrary; for it has an appearance of perfect proof and certainty, and though only an appearance, the fiction, like other fictions, is apt to impose upon the understanding, and lead it into error.

The grand mistake of the syllogistic theory, then, is the notion that we can ever arrive at demonstration in reasonings about matters of fact; and in carrying out this notion, a form of reasoning was invented, (for *invented* is the word) whereby the appearance, and only the appearance of infallibility, was given to an argument. The very perfection of the proof in a regular syllogism shows the futility of the argument; for we know that, except in mathematics, there is no perfect proof; and consequently, the perfection can be only apparent, and therefore, the result of a trick. This trick, as we have seen, is assuming the conclusion in the premises.

That a system of logic, raised on such a basis, should so long have stood its ground, and that even at the present day it should have eminent supporters, is certainly one of the most extraordinary facts in the history of the human mind.

To the name, the truly great name of Aristotle, must chiefly be attributed this long delusion; a man distinguished in so many branches of science, in Metaphysics, Ethics, Politics, Rhetoric, Criticism, and Natural History; the tutor of Alexander, the founder of the peripatetic philosophy. Assuredly, the writings of Aristotle have shed a light on the world; but the great power of the philosopher is chiefly shown in this, that he bewildered it so long.

To take an instance formerly given. Suppose that, either by induction, or otherwise, we have arrived at this general proposition, that

Trade ought to be free:

we may thence infer directly, that

The corn trade ought to be free.

Here the conclusion follows from the premises, follows probably, but not infallibly; for the proposition "trade ought to be free," though *general*, is not stated as *universal*; and therefore there may be circumstances peculiar to the corn trade, which make it an exception to the rule. But this is the natural mode of reasoning. Now, if we wish to convert this into a syllogism, we must state the argument thus:

All trade ought to be free.

The corn trade is a trade:

Therefore, it ought to be free.

Here, by assuming too much, we render the argument insignificant, for we assume the conclusion in the major premiss.

It is a very fair argument to infer, because trade in general ought to be free, that the corn trade ought to be free; it is an argument drawn from a general proposition or a general principle, as the common phrase is; in other words, an instance of deductive reasoning; but it is no argument to say that the corn trade ought to be free, because all trade ought to be free. This is simply a begging of the question; it is to say, that there can now be no dispute about the matter, that it has been already decided. Take another instance. Our general proposition may be,

"A local legislature is advantageous to a country," whence we may infer, that

"A local legislature in Ireland would be advantageous to that country."

This is a fair argument; but, as the proposition pretends not to universality, there may be circumstances peculiar to Ireland, which render the general rule inapplicable; or, on the contrary, there may in this case be circumstances which render a local legislature peculiarly desirable.

When brought to the form of a syllogism, the argument becomes as follows:

Every country is benefited by a local legislature.

Ireland is a country :

Therefore, Ireland would be benefited by a local legislature.

Here, again, it is evident that by assuming too much, we do away with the argument altogether. We prove nothing, we show the probability of nothing; we suppose the question already settled.

Again, supposing ourselves convinced of the truth of this general proposition, that the law ought to favour the equal partition of property among all the children of a family, daughters as well as sons; it may still be a question whether there be any circumstances peculiar to land, which justify an exception: but, if we begin by an universal affirmation, that all property ought to be equally divided, there is an end at once to reasoning.

Hume's famous argument against miracles, which is contained in a single sentence, may be easily reduced to the form of a syllogism in the first figure; and for that very reason it is nugatory. "A miracle is a violation of the laws of nature; and as a firm and unalterable experience has established those laws, the proof against a miracle, from the very nature of the fact, is as entire as any argument from experience can possibly be imagined." In due syllogistic form, the argument would stand thus:

Whatever is opposed to a firm and unalterable experience is unworthy of credit.

But a miracle (being a violation of the laws of nature) is so opposed:

Therefore, a miracle is unworthy of credit.

The fallacy here lies in assuming in the minor premiss, that there is a *firm* and *unalterable* experience against a miracle; for there exists a great deal of testimony for miracles; and until it be proved that all that testimony is false, it cannot be assumed that there is an invariable experience against them; for testimony is indirect experience, and upon it, by far the greater part of our knowledge depends. Even the major premiss may be contested. If by firm and unalterable experience be meant (and what else can be meant?) the experience of ourselves, our ancestors, and all whom we have known or heard of, then those born and bred between the tropics, and who have never wandered from thence, ought not to believe in ice. In fact, there is scarcely any *universal* proposition that may not be contested; and therefore, dialecticians have been obliged, in order not to expose the hollowness of their art, to have recourse to trifling examples, such as, "All men are mortal." James is a man: therefore, he is mortal. "All men are sinners." John is a man: therefore, he is a sinner: where they knew that the major would not be disputed. Aristotle was more wary, for he stuck to letters, and thus concealed the insignificance of examples.

Thus, the major premiss of the syllogism is, in general, either a truism, or an unwarranted assumption; and therefore, though the inference be irresistible, yet the conclusion must be either trifling or uncertain. But, whatever it be, it is no more, as we have already seen, than what was previously known, being assumed in the premises. We cannot, therefore, wonder, that the syllogistic art, in spite of its great pretensions, should have contributed so little (or rather not at all) to the advancement of knowledge.

If the argument of Hume had not laid claim to infallibility, it could not have been reduced to the form of a perfect syllogism. It would have remained a good, but an obvious argument, namely, that prior to the examination of the particular fact, there is a probability, nay, a strong probability, against any one miracle, on account of the general uniformity of nature. But *general* experience could not answer the purpose of an infallible conclusion; and therefore, *unalterable* or *universal* experience was assumed; and it is exactly by reason of this assumption, that the argument becomes reducible to a syllogism, and, as a demonstration, is deceitful.

We have seen that the grand error which lies at the bottom of the syllogistic theory, is the notion that we can ever arrive at demonstration about matters of experience; and in carrying out this notion, it was found necessary to assume, for premises, *universal* propositions instead of *general* ones. This is the precise difference between the ordinary, or natural mode of reasoning, that is, of deductive or general reasoning, and the artificial or syllogistic. We may reason from general propositions, that is, we may attempt to show that any particular case is comprehended under a general truth; but, we cannot reason from universal propositions; for these obviate the necessity of reasoning. We reason in order to prove something not known before; but if it be already known, why reason?

So far concerning deductive reasoning, and the syllogism, the insuperable objection to which last is, that it presents a form of reasoning inapplicable to any real discourse; that, under the semblance of a perfect or infallible argument, it, in fact, does away with all argument.

When I consider the reasons on which this conclusion is built, they appear to me so clear and cogent, that here I could rest in full conviction. But when I reflect on the fact, that for many ages, and throughout all civilized Europe, the syllogism was adopted, and that still some of the greatest thinkers defend it, I am almost tempted to fall back into scepticism, and to discard metaphysics and logic altogether, as destined perpetually to puzzle, never to satisfy mankind. To avoid this scepticism, this unmanly despair, I am forced to rebel against authority, and maintain the liberty of thought.

When men have been wedded to a system, they will not desert it, even when it leads them to absurdities. One might have thought that the following passage was a pretty good refutation of the syllogistic theory of the schools, a real *reductio ad absurdum;* but no, the author adopts the conclusion. "Since all reasoning (in the sense above defined,) may be resolved into syllogisms, and since even the objectors to logic make it a subject of complaint, that in a syllogism the premises do virtually assert the conclusion, it follows at once that no new truth (as above defined) can be elicited by a process of reasoning."[h] Thus, in order to maintain the Syllogistic

[h] Whately's Logic, Book IV. Chap. ii.

Theory, we must allow that no new truth can be elicited by reasoning! The only use of reasoning, then, as we are told, is " to expand and unfold the assertions wrapt up, as it were, and implied in those with which we set out, and to bring a person to perceive and acknowledge the full force of that which he has admitted; to contemplate it in various points of view; to admit in one shape what he has already admitted in another, and to give up and disallow whatever is inconsistent with it."[1] According to this theory, when Pythagoras established by reasoning that, in any right angled triangle, the square of the side subtending the right angle is equal to the squares of the two other sides, he made no discovery, he only unfolded what was before wrapt up in some general notion common to him and other men, some one or more of the mathematical axioms. Must we, then, allow that the above famous proposition is as much contained within the axiom, Things which are equal to the same are equal to one another, or some other similar, as that the proposition, "James is mortal," is contained within " all men are mortal?" No one, not blinded by system, will maintain such a doctrine for a moment. But, the syllogistic theory was to be supported, even at the expense of reason-

[1] Whately's Logic, Book IV. Chap. ii.

ing, which required to be depreciated in order to suit an artificial and futile system.

As reasoning is depreciated in order to suit the syllogistic theory, so are the truths of pure mathematics. We are told that all the propositions of pure mathematics are what Locke calls "trifling," wherein the predicate is merely a part of the complex idea implied by the subject. Thus, when we assert, taking the above example, that in a right angled triangle the square described on the side which subtends the right angle, is equal to the squares described on the two sides containing the right angle, we state merely a trifling proposition, one included in the meaning of the word right angled triangle! If so, it ought to be included in the definition thereof. But the definition says nothing about it. The supposition is evidently preposterous.

Again, the truths of mathematics are represented by the same author, as in conformity, not with the nature of things, but only with our own hypotheses, our own definitions, and therefore comparatively insignificant. There is some foundation no doubt for this statement. The truths of mathematics are not quite conformable to the nature of things; they are strictly true, only on a given hypothesis or definition; but then, they are so far in agreement with the nature of external things, that the nearer things external approach to the things defined, the more nearly does the practical result correspond to the ideal conclusion. Therefore, mathematical truths are not mere ingenious theorems, but pregnant with useful application.

Before me, the author of the Philosophy of Rhetoric, as well as Dr. Thomas Brown, objected to the syllogism, as necessarily involving a *petitio principii*. Dr. Whately does not attempt to prove the contrary, but he answers that the same objection *lies against all arguments whatever*.[k] All arguments involve a *petitio principii!* Am I wrong, then, in saying that all reasoning is depreciated in order to suit an artificial and futile system? After this, I need not add another word upon the syllogism.

V. Thus, we have been able to distinguish three kinds of probable reasoning; the *inductive*, the *deductive*, and the *plain*, of which the two former have more affinity to each other than to the third. We are aware that, according to some, all reasoning is of two kinds, the inductive and the deductive; that one author maintains all probable reasoning to be deductive, or, as he calls it, analytic; and another, that all is inductive.[l]

[k] The words in italics are so printed in the original.

[l] Dr. T. Brown maintains that all reasoning, except the Mathematical, or Proportional, as he calls it, is analytic; while Mr. Mill seems to think that all reasoning is in reality inductive.

But it certainly does not appear from an examination of particular instances, that all probable reasonings can be classed under these two heads, much less all reasonings whatsoever.

Premature generalization is the bane of science; and *principia media* are more applicable and more fruitful than *principia generalissima*. By generalizing prematurely we have always to begin afresh, nothing is gained; whereas, by advancing more cautiously, we establish one position at least, whence we may hope in time to take a higher flight. Bacon has observed, that the grand error of philosophers before his time consisted in this, that from particulars they rose at once to extreme generalities, whence they endeavoured to deduce every thing; whereas, the true method of progress is to advance by degrees from one step of generalization to another, even unto the highest.

Meanwhile, let us examine what relations are the proper subject of each of these sorts of reasoning; for we have seen that all reasoning consists in the tracing of relations.

The subject of demonstrative reasoning is the relations of Quantity and those alone. The first subject of inductive reasoning is the relation of Resemblance, one of amazing extent, by means of which we arrive, also by induction, at the knowledge of other relations, those of Cause and Effect.

The relations traced by deductive reasoning are those of Comprehension, of a whole to a part, as when we show that a particular proposition is comprehended under a general one; the policy of a free trade in corn, for instance, under the policy of free trade in general. Sequences of cause and effect are traced by plain reasoning, as in the examples above given. A is the cause of B, and B of C, therefore, A is the remote cause of C. Relations of Position also are traced by this sort of reasoning, as in the following instance:

York is further from London than Stamford; and Edinburgh is further from London than York; much more then is Edinburgh further from London than Stamford.

From the first proposition, a person totally unacquainted with the position of Edinburgh could infer nothing; and from the second proposition, one unacquainted with the position of Stamford could infer nothing; both, therefore, are necessary to the conclusion, which is not comprehended under either."

" Such relations of Position are, in reality, relations of Quantity, and so, admit of demonstrative reasoning.

VI. It will be observed that we have not attempted, (as some have) to establish an universal principle of reasoning, because we very much doubt whether any such principle exist. We have seen that all reasoning consists in tracing relations, and since these are various, it is natural to presume that the principles of reasoning may be so too. Even in mathematical reasoning, the most simple of any, for it embraces but one kind of relation, clearly distinguished from all other relations, and having its own differences accurately marked out, there is more than one fundamental principle or axiom. Surely then it is unlikely that there can be but one principle for all probable reasoning, which embraces various and complicated relations. The case of mathematics proves, at least, that *all* reasoning is not based upon one principle. "Things which are equal to the same are equal to one another;" and "if equals be added to equals the wholes are equal;" are not one axiom but two.

Do we clearly understand what is meant by a *principle of reasoning?* It is a general truth, of which each inference is a particular instance; a truth either self-evident, as in mathematics, or, at least, to be taken for certain, since it is incapable of proof, and at the same time indispensable to the proof of other propositions. In this, the validity of an inference consists, and upon it, conviction depends. Considered in respect to the reasoning itself, it is an invariable constituent or element; in respect to the influence on the mind, a cause; for, as we have seen,* a principle may be either constituent or elemental, or else causal.

Although we do not pretend to lay down one universal principle of reasoning, yet we may arrive at some general truths on this subject. Since all reasoning consists in tracing relations, and since these are either of coexistence or of succession, it follows that the object of reasoning is to prove either that two or more things coexist or do not coexist; or that two or more things succeed or do not succeed each other; generally, if not invariably. The object of science, in particular, is to determine the permanent or invariable coexistence, and succession of things, partly by direct observation, and where that fails, by reasoning or inference. Where one thing is known certainly to exist, there to expect another along with it; or where one thing is ascertained, to look for another after it; such are the anticipations of human science.

Coexistence and succession being two such different relations, it does seem improbable that

* See Article PRINCIPLE.

the very same maxims of reasoning should apply to both. But let us see whether we cannot determine some which are applicable separately to each.

*Relations of Coexistence:*

Under this head come all the axioms of pure mathematics, which are well known, and therefore, need not here be stated. The following maxims are applicable to other sorts of reasoning.

1. If the first always coexist with the second, and the second with the third, then will the third always coexist with the first.

2. And *vice versa.* If the first never coexist with the second, and if the second always coexist with the third, then will the third never coexist with the first.

*Relations of Succession:*

3. What has been will be.

4. Every effect has a chain of causes.

5. One effect may have many concomitant causes.

6. An effect may be prevented not merely by the absence of the cause or causes proper to it, but also by opposing causes. Therefore, the absence of an *effect* proves not the absence of a *tendency.*

*Maxim applicable to both kinds of Relation:*

7. Two or more things, which resemble each other in many observed particulars, will be found

to agree in other non-observed particulars. From the appearances of agreement we may infer, either that the composition of the things in question is similar, or that the changes which they undergo or produce are similar. The relation of resemblance is peculiar in this, that it may be a relation either of coexistence or of succession; for there may be similarity of sequence as well as of composition.

Relations of resemblance are the foundation not only of all classification, and hence of the descriptive sciences or natural history, but also of reasonings concerning cause and effect, and therefore, of philosophy. Nay, it is the peculiar office of the Imagination to trace relations of resemblance, not so much for the sake of truth, as of effect or emotion. Fortunate, then, is that mind which is alive to relations of resemblance, whether it thread the mazes of science, or follow the flowery paths of eloquence and poetry: and valuable is that memory wherein things suggest others from similarity, and not from mere contiguity in place or in time.

THE END.

Crossley and Billington, Printers, Rugby.

# WORKS BY THE SAME AUTHOR.

## AN ESSAY ON THE DISTRIBUTION OF WEALTH.
8vo. 12s.

## POLITICAL DISCOURSES.
8vo. 9s.

## A DISQUISITION ON GOVERNMENT.
12mo. 4s.

## ANALYSIS AND THEORY OF THE EMOTIONS.
8vo. 6s.

## A CLASSIFICATION OF THE SCIENCES.
4to. 2s. 6d.

EDINBURGH: ADAM AND CHARLES BLACK.
LONDON: LONGMAN, BROWN, GREEN, AND LONGMANS.

## INQUIRY INTO THE PRINCIPLES OF HUMAN HAPPINESS AND DUTY.
8vo. 14s.

LONDON: WILLIAM PICKERING.

www.ingramcontent.com/pod-product-compliance
Lightning Source LLC
Chambersburg PA
CBHW080512090426
42734CB00015B/3033